Cricketers Tales

Collected & edited by
Norman McVicker

Order this book online at www.trafford.com/09-0560
or email orders@trafford.com

Most Trafford titles are also available at major online book retailers.

Note for Librarians: A cataloguing record for this book is available from Library
and Archives Canada at www.collectionscanada.ca/amicus/index-e.html

Printed in Victoria, BC, Canada.

ISBN: 978-1-4269-0005-1

*We at Trafford believe that it is the responsibility of us all, as both individuals
and corporations, to make choices that are environmentally and socially sound.
You, in turn, are supporting this responsible conduct each time you purchase a
Trafford book, or make use of our publishing services. To find out how you are
helping, please visit www.trafford.com/responsiblepublishing.html*

*Our mission is to efficiently provide the world's finest, most comprehensive
book publishing service, enabling every author to experience success.
To find out how to publish your book, your way, and have it available
worldwide, visit us online at www.trafford.com/10510*

www.trafford.com

North America & international
toll-free: 1 888 232 4444 (USA & Canada)
phone: 250 383 6864 ♦ fax: 250 383 6804
email: info@trafford.com

The United Kingdom & Europe
phone: +44 (0)1865 487 395 ♦ local rate: 0845 230 9601
facsimile: +44 (0)1865 481 507 ♦ email: info.uk@trafford.com

10 9 8 7 6 5 4 3 2 1

**Proceeds from the Sale
of this book will be used
to support Junior Cricket
at Cleethorpes Cricket Club**

Preface

Sadly, Norman, who had been planning this book for a long time, did not live to see it through to publication. In many ways it is now a very appropriate memorial to an outstanding cricketer who played it hard, but always in a truly sporting manner, and could always see the humorous side of any situation. I am sure he would have wished me to thank all who are listed in this book; they have contributed hugely to the memory of a very good friend.

Most writers wishing to promote their new book will ask some famous person to write a preface, hoping that such an endorsement will naturally boost sales. The fact that I – honoured though I am – have been given this task can be taken as the first of the scores of jokes, hilarious stories and situations, to be found in this outstanding collection. My own progress to my present position in this Club is nothing short of amazing considering that, as a young member of the 1st XI, once dropped a dolly at cover, and, in my shame and anger, hurled the ball at the stumps, missing them and the keeper by a distance, but hitting the then President at first slip a fearful blow on the ankle.

Cricket seems to produce more anecdotes, comic situations, and downright farce, than all other sports put together. Maybe this is because games last longer; plenty of time for the bizarre and the unexpected to happen. Or maybe it is the enormous number of real characters this wonderful game produces. The bookshelves of the average cricketer are loaded with cricket books; this one should most definitely be squeezed in since it is such a wonderful collection of the sort of memorably amusing moments we have all experienced in one form or another.

Norman cast his net far and wide, making good use of his popularity and well known powers of persuasion. The result will, I am sure, be a fitting memorial to him, and a boost for the promotion of Junior Cricket at Cleethorpes, and something that enhances the great spirit that exists among cricketers.

Ray Mawer
President – Cleethorpes Cricket Club

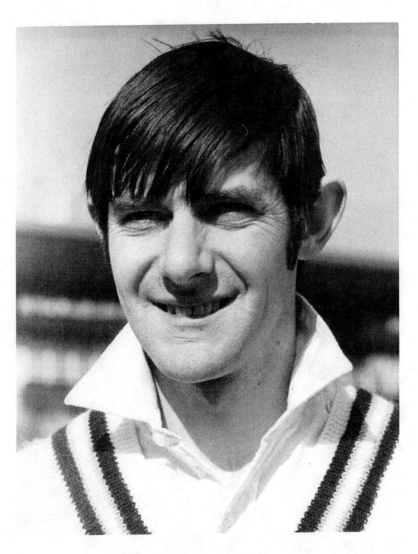

Norman McVicker
1940 – 2008

Norman McVicker

Remember

Oh! The scent of spring time mowing of the cricket
square
Heralding the season, when sound of ball on bat
Will ring loud, and the prospect of sunny days
Cling to the heart.
And Oh! Spare a thought for cricketers past
Who cannot be here today.
Boots whitened, flannels pressed,
Bats oiled, bags packed,
Who would love to play – home or away
But cannot in their shadowy world.
They've had their innings and their seasons
And are faded history
But they smile – and grimace – from old photographs
To remind me to remember them
And play the game as they would play

Ambitions

The length was perfect
With a zip of the seam that left me nowhere
And I nicked it – just a tiny one, mind
And it flew through the air to the keeper behind.
Sadly for him it spilled out.
I thought 'today's just my day'
But the next was a corker – a yorker – sending me on
my way

M J K (Mike) Smith
Leicestershire and Warwickshire CCC, England

'Blowers'

On tour in India in the mid-sixties we woke up on the morning of the Bombay Test with eleven fit players, which included four seamers and two wicketkeepers - Jimmy Binks and Jim Parks. That didn't leave too many batsmen and we soon had one less when I ran out Jim Parks!

On tour then you played as MCC - The Marylebone Cricket Club selected the touring party as opposed to the England selectors. The only other MCC man with any real playing experience was Henry Blofeld; Cambridge blue and out there with the media.

It didn't come to it, but Henry could have been roped in to play. All the others were sick in hospital.

Henry was not often short of a word or opinion, but the prospect of a five-day Test in Bombay quietened him down considerably!

Many rumours were fed to him from other press men and players, and had it not been a Test perhaps we should have got him on the field somehow. Thinking back we should have at least got him changed and really put the pressure on!

****

Eric Sykes CBE
Scriptwriter, Comedian and Actor

'From behind the stumps'
Fred Trueman was being interviewed on radio and when asked, 'Who was the bravest wicket keeper you ever bowled to?' without hesitation he shot back, "Eric Sykes". There was a stunned pause from the interviewer, and then Fred went on, "He stopped every ball with his chest!"
What a bowler and what a joy to be in his company!

****

Norman McVicker.
Lincolnshire, Warwickshire and Leicestershire CCC

'Black and White'
Enter Mike (MJK) Smith at the fall of our second wicket at Old Trafford.
Arriving at the crease Mike asked for his customary guard of 'two' from umpire Bill Alley who was chatting to Peter Lever about a certain social function to be held that evening after close of play. 'Sorry, MJK, just a shade to off, that's it', replied Bill and turned to continue his discourse with Peter, who by now was disappearing into the distance to prepare to bowl his first delivery to MJK. 'Bill, how many balls to come?' queried Mike.
Clive Lloyd was crossing the wicket to take up a customary role at cover point and said, 'There are two balls to go, Michael.' MJK, not convinced, again enquired of the umpire who by now had settled arrangements for the evening's festivities, turned to advise there were two balls left in the over. A voice floated over from cover, 'I hope you're satisfied, Michael, now you have it in black and white!'

****

'Anon'

A cricket club had reached the semi-final of an important knock-out competition and instructed their secretary to meet with his opposite number to agree the venue - home or away.

Arrangements were duly made to meet but for whatever reason he did not turn up to discuss the issue with his counterpart. However, he reported back to his committee that his team would be playing away from home. Apparently he had telephoned the opposing secretary to make his apologies who suggested that as time was short, perhaps they could toss a coin to decide. He thought it a fair compromise and called 'Heads' as the coin was duly tossed at the other end of the 'phone. Back came the answer 'Tails'!

There were more than red faces, as might be understood, on receipt of this news.........!

****

Bill Frindle, MBE
Cricket Statistician, scorer and broadcaster

England's Ashes at Last - 2005!

This series has been hailed as the greatest ever. Ludicrously crammed into the last eight weeks of the longest-ever English first-class season, it was certainly the most tense, exhilarating, emotional and dramatic I have chronicled over the last 40 years.

Even through the early season hype, few expected England to regain The Ashes. Even Duncan Fletcher, England's coach, thought we would have to wait until the 2006-07 series 'down-under' before we might do so.

The Australians were favourites to win the series and reliant almost exclusively on Glenn McGrath and Shane Warne to spearhead their attack. However, McGrath's injury, sustained when I rolled an errant ball under his foot during the first day warm up at Edgbaston, helped ensure the pendulum swung the other way! Ricky Ponting's 'arrogant' decision to bowl first allowed England to reach 407 on that opening day.

Whilst England scraped home by the narrowest Ashes margin of two runs at Edgbaston, on more than one occasion the home side faltered. Losing seven wickets in squeezing 129 to win at Trent Bridge and had Warne not dropped Kevin Pieterson when on 36 on the final morning at The Oval, The Ashes might not have been regained after a wait of over 16 years. Such are the vagaries of the game.

Over-excited scenes in the Test Match Special box during the closing stages of those last four Tests reminded me of the rocket launching control room at Cape Kennedy! Somehow I managed to keep my emotions in neutral and concentrate on my work as scorer. However, it was an immense privilege to have witnessed every ball throughout the series - and from one of the best seats available - as part of a commentary team that, through the wonders of modern technology, was listened to in some of the remotest parts of the world.

****

Bob Leafe
Cricket Chairman, Cleethorpes CC

'The Risk of playing away'

Travelling is always a precarious business when connected with cricket teams.

I have known of a car full of players, who in setting out from Lincolnshire to tour the Isle of Wight, skirted Bristol en- route and enjoyed the delights of the Quantocks.

The reason for this sort of mishap is not necessarily the dullness of the driver, rather the prankish - if not alcoholic - spirit on the part of the navigator. Nor would there be any assistance forthcoming from the rear passengers. Most likely they would be either arguing the 'runs' value of the Coach and Horses, spotting 'birds' or simply comatose.

A favourite story for me relates to a sea journey. For those like myself experiencing sea sickness at the mere sight of water, the crossing of the River Humber by ferry, prior of course to the building of the Humber Bridge, was in fact something of a major voyage. Indeed the trip by the Cleethorpes club to play Hull Y.P.I. across the Humber was a biennial event and an excursion to somewhere completely foreign - Yorkshire.

The trip was always fraught with organizational difficulties, linking the time of start with the tide times, and then the associated timing of the twenty-five mile car journey from Cleethorpes to the New Holland Pier from where the ferry made its two-mile crossing to Hull.

The pier itself was a quarter of a mile long structure stretching outwards across of the Humber and then with a right-angle turn to a berthing jetty in deeper water. Cars would be left at a car park on the terra firma of Lincolnshire, and some way from the ticket office at the entrance to the pier. On making the crossing our hosts would meet us at the Hull jetty and transport us to the Y.P.I. ground.

The visit I recall with some fondness involved us yet again being typically late setting off from Cleethorpes, and belting along the country roads to make the ferry time. We parked up, grabbed our gear, steamed through the ticket office, and ran down the long pier.

My story concerns one Howard Hills, an athletic young man with an impish grin, and for whom nailing one's kit bag to the changing room floor, flying ones underwear from the flagpole, and ejecting bats from car windows was all commonplace. He was affectionately known to have a 'dry' sense of humour!

At the New Holland car park, Howard failed to collect some of his gear from the car boot. These were not the days of 'coffins' or giant bags, let alone with wheels. Dirty boots might be in a carrier bag, separate from 'whites' carried in a hold-all. At the ticket office he realized he needed to return to the car and retrieve the rest of his gear.

By the time Howard returned and emerged from the ticket office, the rest of his team mates were at the other end of the pier, exhorting him above the noise of the ferry's steam funnel

to sprint down the pier as the ferry was about to depart.
Howard turned the corner of the pier to the berthing jetty at full speed. The ship was now a couple of feet from its mooring. He slung the cricket bags over the side of the vessel, then retreated a couple of yards and made a running jump on to deck of the ferry.

After he picked himself up, he was little amused when the rest of his team mates emerged from behind some container boxes stored on the jetty, and to further find that the ferry was coming into its berthing point, having completed a crossing **from** Hull!

****

Lawrie McMenemy MBE
Football manager : Grimsby Town, Southampton,
Northern Ireland and assistant manager England.

'Practice makes perfect'
When I was managing the Northern Ireland side, I was demonstrating the art of set-pieces from the left but found myself short of top players to cross at a certain height - they were all over the place. I called up a young under Twenty-One player, now playing for a top club, who was a bit shy. (Not surprisingly, being thrust into the limelight.) He did very well!
After the session I asked if he practiced in the afternoons. 'After all', I said, 'Even Elton John practices every day.' 'What, taking free kicks?' was his reply!

****

David Shepherd OBE
Artist

'Mistaken identity?'
Not being particularly interested in sport of any kind, I think I have played cricket twice in my life. The first time, I was a snotty-nosed schoolboy aged about five. The second occasion was perhaps more challenging. In the late 1980's a charity cricket match was held at the Officer's Club in Aldershot, to raise money jointly for the Parachute Regiment Association and the Wildlife Foundation that bears my name. Believe it or not, I was asked to captain one of the teams, probably because it was assumed, as many people do, that I was the Bishop of Liverpool!
It was a very nostalgic occasion because Denis Compton, who captained the other team, told me of the historical connections that particular cricket pitch had with him, where he played as the Battle of Britain was taking place overhead - such is the British stiff upper lip!
Anyway, with feelings of sheer terror at the thought of losing my fingers and never being able to paint wildlife again, I approached the wicket and actually hit the first ball. I was so excited I turned round and knocked the bails off, and that was final confirmation that I would never be another David Gower. (A lovely man and a great supporter of the David Shepherd Wildlife Foundation.)

****

'Anon' - and rightly so!

We were playing Macclesfield in a key match in 1960. We had a made decent total but the opposition made good progress and cometh the last over of the game, needed three runs to win.

Fielding at fine leg, but twenty yards in from the boundary, I went to pick up a leg-glance which was an easy single. Sadly for me, somehow, the ball went through my fingers and feet! I turned and chased after the ball. Stooping to retrieve it, I managed to kick it instead - a further five yards towards the boundary. Desperately I set off in hot pursuit and eventually picked it up. Turning to make an arrow-like return to our wicketkeeper - a run-out being our only hope of a tied game - I slipped and fell in what was a soggy outfield. The opposing batsmen had completed the third run to secure victory as my return eventually arrived, to be greeted by a derisory round of applause from my team-mates, even though my mis-field cost us the game!

****

From the Committee Room

The treasurer of one particular club reported to those assembled for a committee meeting that the club had received an anonymous donation of £200 from Eric Jones....!

****

Still Counting!

A batsman was hit full in the box by a fast bowler. He collapsed and had to be assisted from the pitch. The batsman's father, a keen supporter of the club, rushed round the ground and into the pavilion to see how his son was faring after the fearful blow. He said, "That was damned unlucky, so well set with thirty runs under his belt."

"Actually dad, I had scored thirty-seven when I got hit", was his son's agonised reply!

****

Lord Derby

Patron of a cricket club, and elderly, he received a letter from the secretary concerning his patronage. Inadvertently in discreetly mentioning subscriptions/donations would be gratefully received, the secretary enclosed an availability form to cover the first few matches of the season, which was common in those days.
Back came the patron's cheque together with a note from his secretary that his Lordship would not be available for the early matches......

****

Arnie Sidebottom
Yorkshire CCC and England

'Walking on Water'
Geoff Boycott, Ian Botham and the Pope were fishing in the middle of a lake.
At the far corner of the lake was an ice cream van. Botham turned to Boycs and the Pope and said, "Do you fancy an ice cream?" So Botham got out of the boat and walked over the water, bought the ice creams and walked all the way back.
About an hour later, Boycs thought he should do the decent thing and got out of the boat, walked across the water, bought more ice creams and returned.
After a further hour the Pope thought he should return the hospitality and stepped out of the boat. There was a big splash and he sank to the bottom of the lake.
Botham turned to Boycs and said, 'Didn't you tell him about the stepping stones?' Boycs replied, 'Stepping stones? What stepping stones?!!'

****

Stand CC

'Better Safe than Sorry -Take the Mangle'
My brother was captain of the 2nd X1. The side had performed very well throughout the summer and it was a close-run thing as to which of the top sides would win the league title with just a couple of fixtures remaining. Meeting at the club with the other players - an away game against Glossop - my brother suggested to others in the team that as the weather had been wet and windy all week and the Glossop ground was not renowned for any drying facilities, it would be a tragedy if the match was rained off or seriously interrupted by the weather to thwart the team's ambitions for the title.
The Stand club had recently acquired some excellent sacking, wonderful for drying areas of the square, bowlers' ends etc and

my brother suggested they take the sacking along, adding that as he had an estate car, there might be room for the mangle which was used to squeeze water from the sacking during mopping up operations. The mangle, a heavy old-fashioned affair with wooden rollers and a hefty turning handle was duly removed from the groundsman's store, loaded into the car and the team set off for Glossop.

As it turned out, the weather held fair, the mangle was not required, the game was duly won to clinch the title - but it was the first time I had ever heard of a cricket XI taking their own pitch-drying equipment to an away match!

****

Norman McVicker

'A Battle with the Red Rose - and my maiden fifty'
Old Trafford 1972. Believe it or not I joined Rohan Kanhai with our total at 204 for 5. We added 143 in our partnership before Rohan was caught behind off Peter Lee for 199. (Didn't know whether to say well played or bad luck, as he left the crease after a wonderful innings!)

By this time the second new ball had been taken and Lever, Shuttleworth and Lee could be a handful on any wicket. I faced Shuttleworth and as he obligingly pitched a couple of deliveries well up, looking for some swing, I equally obligingly drove them through the covers for boundaries which attracted quite a few less than friendly comments from the bowler. I thought, "Watch out for the next, it won't be in your half!" It wasn't! I was already seeking refuge on the pitch as the ball left his hand. Somehow, as I hit the deck, I left my bat in the air (bit like a periscope, I suppose) and the ball hit some part of it before sailing clean over Engineer's head behind the stumps and only failing to register a six by a couple of yards. Well, the air turned blue and I could tell Shuttleworth was not best pleased!

However I rode it out, but not before returning for a second run off Peter Lee a couple of overs later, I found myself bundled out of my ground by Farokh who had received the return from the outfield and in his most friendly manner (a wonderful man and a good sportsman) pretended to take off the bails to claim a run-out.

It was during the same innings that I got a thin edge to Peter Lever, snapped up by Farokh with a triumphant appeal. 'Not out', was the umpire's reply. It was the last ball of the over and as Farokh passed me, I said, 'Rookie, that ball bounced before you caught it.' 'I know', he replied, 'But it only just bounced...!'

Those were the days......

******

'An original thigh pad design'
I was intrigued by Mike (MJK) Smith's thigh pad when I first went to Edgbaston. This long before the days of helmets, arm-guards and various other body armour as fast bowlers were still aiming at the stumps.(You used to stuff a towel round your jockstrap and it did the job reasonably well!)

Mike's creation comprised a section of a plastic bucket (sliced vertically) with a cushion of 'buffalo' mat applied within the bucket section and sewn to the plastic, the whole being enclosed in a pillow case complete with tapes to hold the contraption in place when positioned. The shape of the bucket would fit neatly round the wearer's thigh and almost guaranteed at least one leg-bye when struck by a fast bowler, the ball flying over the head of the short square leg fieldsman!

I thought this invention a good idea, bought the other half of the bucket and mat and copied his idea. It worked!

****

'How's That!'
Batting against Kent, I nudged Bob Woolmer to gully where Colin Cowdrey scooped up and claimed a slightly dubious

catch. I was not entirely convinced, but without looking at the umpire I asked him if he had taken it cleanly. 'I think so, Norman', was his reply, whereupon I immediately left the crease.

Returning to the pavilion, 'MJK', our captain asked if I had waited for the umpire's decision. I replied, 'No. Colin said he had made the catch and that was good enough for me.'

Mike's reply was, 'Fair enough', and that was the end of the matter. I think somewhere in this story is a message about the spirit of the game of cricket.........

****

'The Maestro'

With a couple of wickets under my belt and bowling to Gary Sobers when he was playing for Nottinghamshire at Trent Bridge - he was batting pretty well and I was confident of my bowling - I thought, "I'll let him have one!" In went the bouncer, the ball disappeared over the Ladies' pavilion and I never bowled another short delivery to the great player again!

****

'Ave'

At a gathering of former Warwickshire cricketers at Edgbaston for a reunion, I was pleased indeed to see Bill Blenkiron, a quick bowler and former team-mate. Having a jar and chat together before lunch in the committee-room, he told me he had only been in the room once before and that was when the club sacked him!

Steve Rouse (Rebel), now head groundsman at Edgbaston, told me of the occasion when he was sacked. Steve was built like a brick outhouse and immensely strong, but seemed to spend a lot of time in the treatment room during his time on the playing staff as a more than useful seamer. He informed me he was told over a pint of beer in Blackpool during an away match his contract would not be renewed!

In those days there was a large clipboard outside the changing rooms where in-coming post for the players was placed. At end of season, there were always one or two players with a wary eye on the board, as contracts became renewable. If you received one size A4, you were safe for another year or two. A smaller envelope meant you would be clearing out your locker and leaving the playing staff.

****

'Bill and Rebel'
At a gathering of former Warwickshire cricketers at Edgbaston for a reunion, I was pleased indeed to see Bill Blenkiron, a former quick bowler and team-mate. Having a jar and chat together before lunch in the committee-room, he told me he had only been in the room once before and that was when the club sacked him!
Steve Rouse (Rebel), now head groundsman at Edgbaston, told me of the occasion when he was sacked. Steve was built like an out-house and immensely strong, but seemed to spend a lot of time in the treatment room. He informed me he was told over a pint of beer in Blackpool during an away match his contract would not be renewed!
In those days there was a large clipboard outside the changing rooms where in-coming post for the players was placed. At end of season, there was always a wary eye on the board, as contracts became renewable. If you received one size A4, you were safe for another year or two. A smaller envelope meant you would be clearing out your locker and leaving the playing staff.

****

MEJC (Mickey) Norman
Northamptonshire and Leicestershire CCC

Playing Glamorgan at Cardiff and in company of McVicker - we did win the game - bumped into Ossie Wheatley, former fast bowler for Warwickshire and the home county. In discussion it transpired Ossie was supplying the local University with wines and spirits. My ears pricked up at this revelation and asked if he could supply me with a couple of cases. McVicker, circumspectly, opted for one mixed case.

The wine was duly delivered the following morning and we loaded the cases into the boot, having settled a modest bill for such generosity. We travelled home, having trusted Ossie's judgement and agreed to open a bottle and compare notes the following day before the start of the next match.

Well! The exchange of comments was brief: 'We know what it is.....but whose!'

(McVicker would add he gave away one bottle as a raffle prize to a local 'good cause' but it was returned unopened with a short note: 'We've tried this before!'

****

John H Edrich MBE
Norfolk and Surrey CCC, England

'Keeping your eye on the game'
Surrey were playing Northants at Guildford. I was batting with Alan Butcher. Colin Milburn was bowling and I was at the non-striker's end. (This was after Colin made a come-back to county cricket, having lost an eye in an horrific car accident.)

Colin, besides being a very attractive and hard-hitting batsman was a useful medium-pace bowler and was bowling from my end. After two or three deliveries he suddenly stopped and exclaimed, 'I have lost my eye!' Sure enough when I looked at him he had, indeed, only one eye.

We proceeded to look around the crease and found it lying on the ground - the false eye glaring up at us on discovery. Colin picked it up, pocketed it and continued to bowl!

Colin Milburn was a wonderful cricketer, one of the game's great characters, and it was a tragedy when his cricketing career was brought to a premature, abrupt end.

****

Jack Bannister
Warwickshire CCC. Journalist and Radio/TV
commentator

'Woof! Woof!'

Sydney, New Year Test 1983. England, having won the previous match at Melbourne by the very tightest of margins, were 2-1 down and desperately needed to win in Sydney to draw the series.

That well known and inspirational England captain, Bob Willis, gave them everything Shakespeare ever wrote for King Henry V at Agincourt as a pre-match gee-up, plus a few phrases of his own. The gist was an early wicket.

England fielded first. Willis bowled the first ball to Keppler Wessels with John Dyson at the non-striker's end. In that first over, Wessels dabbed straight back to Willis and called Dyson for the all-time suicidal single.

Willis pounced to his left, turned round with a turning circle marginally quicker than QE2, and threw down the stumps. Umpire Mel Johnson at square leg had no distraction.. Short leg had chased the ball, keeper Bob Taylor was only half-way to the stumps and Dyson yards away.

'Not out', was his verdict. The Sydney evening newspaper pictured the Channel 9 freeze-frame with only the tip of Dyson's bat in view - and at knee-height - as he was not close enough to run it in. The run-out distance was calculated at 3'9".

Johnson now knew he had a problem and called a press conference at close of play. He said, 'It was 6 inches either way and too close to call.' Aussie journalist Phil Wilkins knocked on the England dressing room door and asked for Doug Insole - never short of wit.

Wilkins: 'Manager; Johnson says 6 inches either way is too close to call.' Insole, just before he closed the door replied, 'I assume he is talking about LBW's!'

Not a bad punch line, but the better appeared in the following morning's Sydney broadsheet. Their cartoon had Johnson with white stick, dark glasses and guide dog, bowler and non-striker looking at him and the caption in the bubble said, "Now remember, it's one woof for out and two for not-out."

****

David Lloyd
Lancashire CCC, England

Many years ago when I was still playing, I was having a chat with my Yorkshire mate Geoff Boycott.

I innocently asked him if he had been scoring many lately.

He was straight in. 'I always score runs', he replied, 'although I had a rough time last week. I was batting against that Geoff Arnold at Surrey - medium out-swing. I played when I needed to, left most of 'em round off-stump. I had him lined up, all worked out.

He then bowled an absolute snorter. Swung in, pitched, nipped away and caught me a bit square on. I tried to leave it but it did me. I nicked it and was caught behind. ......(pause)...... An ordinary player like you would have missed it......!'

****

Ken Roberts
Stand CC

'Many a Slip'

Playing for Stand at Levenshulme in a Lancs. and Cheshire League game on a typical

Manchester summer day - very wet, the pitch all mud and sawdust - I opened the bowling and 'racing' in to bowl, slipped in the delivery stride. All bowlers know that when this occurs the ball is pitched short - one side of the wicket or the other!

This one was on the off-side. The batsman hammered the ball into the covers. The non-striker set off for what he thought a comfortable run. The ball flew straight to cover, an excellent fielder, who picked it up and returned it to the wicket-keeper.

Both batsmen were now at the same end - both 'in' - and the 'keeper, in possession, lobbed the ball to me - I had taken up the post of guarding the stumps at the other end - which went way over my head. With eyes glued on the ball, I back-pedalled as fast as I could, leapt up, caught the ball, and in a swift movement dived headlong through all the mud and sawdust, removing the bails and letting out an ear-piercing appeal.

By this time the batsman who was backing up had given up his cause and was half-way back to the pavilion.

I had made a bit of a fool of myself, much to the amusement of my colleagues!

Moments later a boundary was scored which finished in a cabbage patch next to the pavilion. Running to retrieve the ball and taking a short-cut, I went to jump a spectator bench, missed and fell headlong into the cabbage patch.

This was too much for a team-mate who remarked, 'By 'eck, his third trick will be a bloody good un!

****

Brian D ('Bomber') Wells
Gloucestershire and Nottinghamshire CCC

'Twice is enough......'
I was a mere lad of sixteen and turning out for the Nondescripts - 'The Nondies' - a Bristol-based nomadic club. Witney (Oxon) was one our precious venues.
On this particular day I was bowling and taken a wicket when in strode Len Herrings, who had quite a reputation as a batsman. He took what seemed for ever to take guard and look round the field. My first delivery was too good for him and he was bowled.
At slip was Bill Hook - he was the England full-back at the time, as well as the Gloucester club and county player - who called out to our skipper Jack Stephens (who was the first rugby union player to turn professional) 'I don't think he was looking when Bomber bowled.' (It is a fact 'Bomber' had the shortest run up to the wicket in the history of the game - three paces on a good day!)
Jack was thinking we might lose the fixture if what Bill said was true - it was a lovely ground and setting - and asked Bill to go after him and persuade him to return to the crease. After some minutes of discussion in the pavilion, both Bill and Len returned to the field. Len to the crease and Bill to slip.
He took guard again and I asked him if he was ready this time. He replied he was. I bowled him again, first ball.
He pushed himself up straight then very calmly said to Bill Hook, 'If you think I'm staying here for a bloody 'hat-trick' you've another thought coming! I'm away', and off he went shaking his head......

****

Frederick Sewards Trueman OBE
Yorkshire CCC, England

'A recollection of the Reverend David Sheppard'
'We were playing a Test match at Brisbane with a capacity crowd. Sadly, David had had a miserable tour in respect of catches - in fact he had not caught a thing - and was posted to the outfield when Fred Titmus came on to bowl his off-spinners.

Brian Booth was batting (a lay preacher and a nice man, too) and decided to have a 'dart' at Fred. He struck the ball high and far in the general direction of the 'Reverend', who had to make a lot of ground to attempt a catch. He did, much to his own delight, and joyously tossed the ball high in the air in front of the Australian crowd and in the light of earlier failures took a bow!

Brian Statham was the nearest of the England fielders to David Sheppard and shouted to him, 'For goodness sake, get the ball back. It was a no-ball and they've already run five!'

****

Peter Walker
Glamorgan CCC, England

'The pain of being a cricket coach'
Like many English county cricketers I used to spend winters coaching in South Africa, a country I knew well having grown up there.

My main employers were the Transvaal Cricket Union and I was given a Rota which took me around the Johannesburg area. Young men of those days were no different to those now, their attention spans barely stretching beyond five minutes. Running two nets with eight boys in each inevitably meant that I couldn't give each lad the attention he deserved so once, as a lad swished away across the line of the ball but rarely making contact, the bowlers standing around starting to lose interest, I knew I had to do something unusual to grab their attention.

I went down to the batsman, asked him to step to the side of the net and pulled out the middle stump from the ground. Using it as a bat, I took my stance at the crease. I looked up at the lads waiting to bowl. 'OK let it go as fast as you like'. (Remember I had no pads, box or gloves on.)

The first few lads sent down gentle medium paced deliveries all of which I hit smack in the middle of the stump before turning to the watching batsman with the words, 'See, it is possible to hit the ball but you must play straight, don't cow-shot it over mid-wicket. Watch again.'

The bowling fraternity had obviously been impressed so they launched their 17 year old 6'4" fast bowler to 'let the coach have one.' At around 80 mph it pitched outside the off stump and jagged back into me from the coconut matting to hit me smack of the left shin bone!

The pain was excruciating but I knew I dare not show this to the young lads. I stood aside for the batsman and walked out of the net trying not to hobble.

When the session ended 20 minutes later and the boys had gone, I tentatively lifted my trouser leg. There was an enormous lump with the seam mark prominent. A 'war wound' which I carry, thankfully not so big, to this day 50 years on.

Is there a cricketing motto to this story? What about, 'Think before you do something stupid!'

****

Roy Oslear
Cleethorpes CC

'The road to success?'

John Watson of Sleaford was a fine cricketer who appeared for Lincolnshire and a great character.

In those days of friendly cricket, now many years ago, Sleaford, Wisbech and Bourne presented Cleethorpes most competitive but enjoyable fixtures in the South of the county.

Involved in this tale is our own Paul Gregory, who also played for Lincolnshire. Paul was always very competitive and entered many a personal battle with members of the opposition, often spicing up dull matches. Some he won, some he lost. This was one he lost.

John was not noted as a batsman but belonged to the school of big hitting tail-enders.

On one occasion he 'got lucky' and carted Paul for several big sixes into the garage block at the far end of the ground.

The following year we noticed a housing development taking place where the garages had been situated, and this was casually commented upon in the bar after the match in a conversation with John.

'Yes', he said thoughtfully puffing his pipe, 'The local council were very good and came to us and asked if we had any ideas for street names. I told them they should call the nearest road beyond the fence Gregory Way and the one beyond that Gregory Further Away!

****

Dave Boylen
Grimsby Town Football Club

'Amusing times at Blundell Park'

Under Lawrie McMeneny's management, it was a custom to undertake a run along the beach down to the Winter Gardens, have a coffee, then run back, have a shower and a team talk about how we would approach the game on Saturday.

This certain day, some bright spark was looking out of the window of the Winter Gardens as we enjoyed our coffee and noticed that the No. 4 bus was there, ready and waiting. So, quickly finishing our refreshment we climbed aboard for an easy ride back to the ground. Not a wise move when Lawrie is in charge! He had spies everywhere, even on the bus leaving the Winter Gardens with twenty-odd players aboard. There we were all laughing and joking that we had put one over on the trainer, Jim Clunie, who had decided to go back to the ground to help Lawrie with selection and the team meeting.

The other passengers thought it hilarious to see their idols on a bus going to the football ground. We thought it was great, signing autographs and laughing and joking with everyone on board. Then, horror of horrors, Dave Worthington, who was captain of the team at the time, as we approached the stop nearest the Blundell Park Hotel shouted out, 'The boss is at the shelter.' We all thought he was joking but, no, the big man - all six-foot-seven of him - was waiting for the bus to stop.

There was no escape! We had been caught out and what he had to say was brief as each player dismounted. He fined each and every one of us £10 - a considerable sum in those days - and made it plain to the other passengers who was in charge!

In later years he told us he knew within five minutes of us getting on that bus he was contacted and that was why he was waiting to 'greet' us!

We all had to run again to the Winter Gardens - and back to Blundell Park - as a penance. This time, we did not even get a cup of coffee!

****

'The Artie White Foundation'

During my time with the foundation, I have managed to attract some big names to our gatherings - Bobby Charlton, Norman Whiteside, Nobby Stiles, Jack Charlton, Geoff Hurst, Denis Law being but a few.

On one occasion at the Winter Gardens I had arranged to pick up Denis from the Hotel Elizabeth. On arrival Denis suggested we discuss the itinerary over a drink at the bar.

As we stood there overlooking the golf course with a wedding reception having taken place, photographs were being taken of the wedding party on the lawn. The groom could not believe his luck, being an avid Manchester United fan, recognizing Denis through the windows and asked if he would be good enough to join those assembled on the lawn. He readily agreed and took his place. A photograph for posterity!

A perfect gentleman who helped make the groom's day in more than one way(?) and the evening dinner a huge success.

****

David Gower OBE
Leicestershire, Hampshire CCC. England

'Just a cricketing tale'
On the tour of India in '84-85 which I captained, thankfully to success, one of my selections was Chris Cowdrey, a long standing close friend and a very good man to take on tour anywhere. After all, if you can't pick your mates who can you pick? He was selected mainly with the one day matches in mind but actually played in all five tests. Well someone had to stand at short leg to Edmonds and Pocock!

Just before the touring party was due to depart, Chris rang me in a bit of a quandary, to say that he had picked up an injury during training and had 'done' a hamstring. As this would prevent him bowling for a while he thought he ought to do the decent thing and ring his captain. 'Should I offer to pull out of the tour?' he suggested. 'Don't be daft', I said, 'It doesn't matter to me if you can't bowl. You can't get out of it that easily - you are coming.'

So he eased himself through those first couple of weeks of the tour without having to exert himself unduly, doing just enough gentle batting in the nets to keep himself going and in due course found himself in the test team up against India's finest.

The first test did not go our way in Bombay, where we were ambushed by a little wrist spinner by the name of Laxman Sivaramakrishnan. At least we picked ourselves up and fought back later to win the series but that match in Bombay was a bit of a struggle. It eventually got to the stage where I thought I could even give Chris a bowl, but not until we had a bit of a crisis on our hands and the front-line attack was struggling for a break through.

The moment came for me to throw him the ball as our main

bowlers began to feel the heat, with Kapil Dev in full flow. I set the field with men in the deep everywhere, myself at extra cover so I could maintain contact with Chris as he bowled his first balls in test cricket, with just one slip, Mike Gatting, the definition of a stout man if ever there was one! I might just add that Mike was about to have a marvelous tour and made a fine hundred in the second innings and indeed scored a wonderful double hundred in the Madras test which later won us the series.

Anyway, back to the first innings in Bombay. England all out 195 and India now 218 for 5. After a couple of dot balls as Kapil sized him up, I wandered across and asked Chris if he was happy with the field, and suggested that maybe he would like 'Gatt' a bit wider at slip. Chris's immediate response: 'If he gets any wider he'll burst!'

When, two balls later, Chris delivered the perfect inswinger and bowled Kapil none of us was more surprised than Chris, or for that matter his father, Colin, later Lord Cowdrey, who was listening to the commentary on his car radio back in London and apparently promptly drove the wrong way down a one way street.

The copper who spotted him refused to believe such an unlikely tale either and promptly nicked him!

****

Judge Michael Heath

'Albert'
The legendary Albert Peart's dexterity behind the stumps - and indeed between the goal posts - was not entirely matched by his facility with the English language.
Captaining Ross Sports 2nd X1 on one occasion he announced to his team: 'I've lost the toss and we've been injected!'

****

'Promotion in the batting order? No thank you captain'

I played for Normanby Park Works against Sheffield United in a national knock-out competition. They hit us all over for 280 in 45 overs!

My usual batting berth was at number six. Our captain invited me to open our reply and I leapt at the chance. When I got to the crease I realized why I had been chosen to open. I have never seen a wicket-keeper stand so far back. I needed binoculars to discern his face! The bowler was black and bespectacled. I stereotyped him as probably being a medical student at Sheffield University.

He had a slow and mazy run to the wicket but the first ball he bowled to me was the fastest I have ever faced!

It pitched just short of a length and fizzed past my nose. Had I batted right handed it could have killed me.

So alarmed was our number three that he went behind the pavilion to be sick! The second ball was a huge wide, the third a very short bouncer. The fourth was a full toss which struck my bat and went in the direction of cover point. The non-striker was insistent that we run two! I survived the rest of the over.

I then reflected that this was only time on a sports field I had been concerned for my personal safety. I did not own a helmet - in those days they tended only to be worn by batsmen in the first class game - my fellow opener wore plimsolls and had no thigh pad! I thought of my dependant wife and two small sons at home.

I faced up to the third over. The first two deliveries were huge wides. The third was a straight yorker. Its straightness surprised me, given what had gone before. I jabbed my bat down. The ball hit the toe of my bat and rolled towards the stumps. (It was so windy we had dispensed with bails.) The ball rolled gently against the base of the stumps. I turned to leave the crease. In one the most unwelcome displays of sportsmanship I have ever encountered, the wicket-keeper shouted, 'You're not out, mate. The ball would not have knocked off the bails!'

I retorted, 'It's near enough for me!' and made my way back to the pavilion as fast as I could.

That was my one and only meeting with Devon Malcolm, then an occasional Derbyshire 2nd XI player.

****

'Didn't know an Arse from an Elbow'

Bowlers' familiarity with laws of the game are variable. Batting at Hykeham one day,

a ball passed down the leg-side, hit my ample backside and was caught by the diving wicket-keeper. The bowler was dismayed when his enthusiastic appeal for 'caught behind' was rejected by the umpire.

I got a single off the next ball and said to the bowler, 'that one before hit me on the backside.' 'I'm sorry', he said, 'I thought it hit you on the elbow!'

****

Neal Abberley
Warwickshire CCC

'Running between the wickets'

My first year on the playing staff and eager to impress the coach. I ran out the senior player, Basil Bridge - an off-spinner and middle-order batsman who had taken 134 wickets for the county the previous year - at Stratford in a 2nd XI game - but now struggling to regain his place in the 1st XI and desperate for runs to hasten a recall.

Having lost a couple of early wickets Basil strode to the wicket. The bowler was Ted Hemsley with the 'keeper standing up to the stumps with three slips behind him. Basil wore enormous pads and thrust out to his first delivery which hit him on the pad. Loud appeal from all around. Even today I recollect the ball flying past Alan Ormrod at slip. I called for a run and Basil set off like a greyhound out of the traps!

I took two or three paces and stopped in horror as I saw the ball six inches from the stumps. Basil, by this time, was ten yards up the pitch. Result: Basil run-out by ten yards for nought!

Tom Dollery, our coach, was not amused and shut all the changing room windows! I was not looking forward to going back to the pavilion and managed to score a century. The only words from Tom were, 'It was a good job you did.'

It cost me a few pints to placate Basil.

****

'Sunday League match v Sussex at Hove'

The player's balcony is situated high up in the pavilion giving a good view of the ground from square leg. The pitch on this occasion was close to the pavilion leaving a long boundary on other side. Towards the sea-end of the ground there is a slope and the ground falls away quite a lot.

I middled a shot in that direction on the on-side and thought it a definite boundary. Running the customary first run with my opening partner, Billy Ibadulla, we stopped and had a chat in the middle of the wicket as John Snow ambled round to retrieve the ball which, out of sight, I was sure was a four. We were wrong! 'Snowy' collected the ball and lobbed it 50 yards to another fielder who, appraising the situation with the two of us discussing whatever came to mind, targeted the bowler's end with a strong throw.

I said to Billy, 'I think you'd better get back - and quick!' Too late! He was run-out by half a street as the ball -out of our sight - had not crossed the boundary.

Alan Smith, our captain, watching from on high with other members of our side was not amused, but saw the funny side later that evening after we had won the match.

****

Don Oslear
Cleethorpes CC and former First Class/Test umpire

Views from 22 yards - or thereabouts.

Over more than 60 years of participation in various sports at amateur, semi-professional and full-time professional levels, I have viewed many incidents from a distance of twenty-two yards - or thereabouts.

Brilliant, tragic, frightening, many more adjectives could be used but the funniest incident must be the one which happened whilst I was playing in goal at soccer. It took place on a ground in South Yorkshire one muddy Saturday afternoon. My side were winning by two or three goals when, very close to full-time, our opponents were awarded a direct free kick just outside our penalty area. Very dutifully, four defenders made a 'wall' and in those days the ball was generally struck with great force at those four bodies. I could never see their faces but some of the vocabulary used, noises emitting from and attitudes and postures adopted by the occupants of that 'wall' defy description. This day I was amazed to see one of our opponents forcing himself into the middle of the 'wall' and even more amazed when the defenders not only allowed him in, but linked arms around his waist to see he remained in that position. The reason soon became clear, for when the kicker was six or seven yards from the ball, the two on either side of the opponent put thumbs in the waistband of his shorts and quick as a flash slid his shorts down to his ankles. From my position not a pretty sight from twenty-two yards or thereabouts!

****

Perhaps one of the most awesome sights or sounds, or should I say the lack of it, is remembered from my ice hockey days. Again I played in goal, or to use the correct term, as net-minder. For certain breaches of the law a penalty shot was awarded. There were two ways this shot could be taken. The one similar to soccer was when the puck was placed on the defence line, which on my home rink was fifteen yards from the goal. The taker of the shot would skate the full length of the rink at an increasing speed, the hubbub of noise rose until he was some four to five yards from the puck and the noise stopped abruptly, like a door being closed on a music room. The only sound to be heard was the rasp of skates on the ice and the expulsion of air from the skater. As the attacker made his shot, which travelled at over 100mph, a net-minder needed not only a steady hand and eye, but also the nerve to catch or deflect the puck from its path into his net. The attacker could also arrive at the puck with great speed, and with his stick bring the puck forward and endeavour to beat the net-minder by taking it around him, or shooting from any position on the way, all the time in dead silence. Should the net-minder block the attempt or the shot with legs, body or hand, or the shot hit the back of the net, the erupting noise from two or three thousand throats in an enclosed arena was like an explosion, but it was the complete silence that descended on the rink for the skater's last twenty-two yards or thereabouts, that I found the most awesome

****

During the years 1972-93 whilst being engaged as a first class umpire, I was privileged to see in action most of the greats of the game of cricket. Some of the names of my umpiring colleagues, great cricketers in their own right before turning to the umpiring profession, included Bill Alley, Ces Pepper and John Langridge. Also two umpires who were regarded as two of the best in the world, David Constant and Harold Bird. Whilst the 2006 season will be my 64th connected with the Cleethorpes club, the experience which I gleaned from all my umpiring colleagues has and will continue to stand me in good stead.

I regret not having started my umpiring career earlier. Not

being able to say that I umpired when such players as Barrington and May, Trueman and Statham, Compton and Edrich were playing, I consider myself fortunate that Colin Cowdrey's last season, 1975, was my first. Fortunate, because I can say that I stood and watched one of the world's great batsmen from a distance of twenty-two yards. Fortunate, too, because my years as a first class umpire spanned the exact years as those of the great Ian Botham, and fortunate to be able to say that whilst the twenty-two yards was a privileged position from which to watch his many match winning feats, they were far too close when he hit one of his drives back toward me, but again fortunate to state he never hit me!

****

One of the most frightening sights must have been of Wayne Daniel of Middlesex in full cry. I umpired a Benson & Hedges match at Hove in 1978 and Wayne was bowling from my end, down the hill with a steady breeze behind him. The pitch was hard and he really wanted to bowl. When he came past me, it was like an express train coming out of a tunnel and he was knocking stumps out of the ground and depositing them fifteen yards back! If anyone had ever bowled faster than he did on that day, it must have been long before my time. I am very pleased that I was taking part as an umpire and not as a batsman. The twenty-two yards must have seemed like twenty-two feet to them!

****

It is common knowledge that I have no first class cricketing background. Indeed I do not have any claim to fame as a cricketer, except a safe pair of hands. I loved to chase, field, throw and most of all catch a cricket ball. You can imagine the thrill I had observing the wonderful fielding and catching skills over twenty-one years at first class level - there were far too many to list. Whilst I have no recollection of the best of all, some of them have been taken in the amateur games in which I have umpired.

****

I expect to have to come back to the batsmen for my most common view from twenty-two yards. The skills of many almost defy description. In 1975 I saw Geoff Boycott bat for one hundred overs of a first innings. He scored 201 not out, never gave a chance and, as I recall, never had an appeal made against him. He came out to bat in the second innings and was out in the first over for a duck. How kind and how cruel the game can be!

Cricket, whilst a team game, is all about individual efforts. A batsman facing a top class spinner, surrounded by close fielders and on a wearing pitch, has no one to help him. Possibly the view from twenty-two yards makes the lasting impression as his judgment of feet and bat in relation to the pitch of the ball has to be so precise.

****

My final memories of those whom I have admired from a distance of twenty-two yards must be reserved for one of our own club members, the compiler/editor of this 'must read' publication, Norman McVicker.

I have always felt that the best situation of a cricket match is to observe the fighting spirit of those who give more than 100% of their ability. In 1975, the season Leicestershire won the First Class Championship for the first time in the club's history, I was appointed to more of my fair share of Leicester matches and our paths crossed many times during that summer. Although he took 46 Championship wickets, it was not as a bowler that I remember him best. Kent v Leicestershire at Tunbridge Wells. Leicester in their first innings were 115 for 8, not even in sight of a batting bonus point, when Norman was joined by Graham McKenzie. Their unbroken stand of 136 for the ninth wicket took the score to 251, whereupon Ray Illingworth immediately declared having claimed three bonus points. Norman's 83 not out was certainly a match winning innings. I viewed him for most of that first day with admiration from a distance of twenty-two yards, unlike the first time we met.

Batting for Cleethorpes against Ross Sports, there were three balls to face and four runs required to win when I took guard. That first ball from Norman struck me very hard in the 'nasty place' with such a clatter it was heard on the Fish Dock in Grimsby!

How I made my perambulation over those twenty-two yards I shall never know..... Perhaps an opportune moment to close my contribution because those who read it will probably state, 'This is a load of b------- anyway!'

****

Dennis Amiss MBE
Warwickshire CCC and England

'Many a slip'
Warwickshire playing Hampshire at the old Army & Navy ground in Portsmouth.

We lost the toss and fielded. Norman Gifford was our captain. During the morning session Gladstone Small bowled particularly well without reward, mainly due to D L Amiss (aged 42) dropping two catches off his bowling at first-slip.

Mid-off was heard to remark, 'Get that old bugger out of there captain. I'll go there and catch everything for you.' (Mid-off was Andy Lloyd, who duly took up my position and I was banished to the outfield.)

After half-an-hour of nothing coming our way, Norman Gifford decided a bowling change was necessary and duly put himself on with his slow left armers.

His third ball was a little short outside off-stump and the batsman slashed at it, getting a top edge. The ball sped to Andy

Lloyd at slip who stood, as was his wont, with hands on knees as it hit him straight on the nose and mouth. He went backwards with hands still on knees, blood spurting everywhere and in a great deal of pain as you can imagine.

Everyone gathered around and you always get the wags in the side (Oh! Bad luck Andy.......great effort Andy.......) to which Andy's reply is unprintable!

The captain arrived to view the casualty and remarked, 'Well Andy, at least Dennis gets a hand on them.!'

****

Jim Cumbes
Lancashire, Surrey, Worcestershire and Warwickshire CCC

'My grandfather remembers you'

Twenty20 at Old Trafford. I had been out in the car park prior to the players arriving for the match and my return to the pavilion was stopped by a young lad, who could only have been 7 or 8 years old at most, who asked for my autograph. I explained I wasn't a player but that they would be arriving shortly if he wanted to wait. However, he insisted I sign his book. After signing and patting him on the head I said, 'I suppose it was your father who remembers me and knows who I am'.

He replied, 'I don't know about that - but my grandad does!'

As you might imagine, it caused much mirth at the time and plenty since!

****

In my days with Surrey, I was bowling against Kent at the Oval with Dickie Bird umpiring at my end - a man I generally got on with pretty well. I was bowling to Brian Luckhurst and had a couple of lbw shouts against him during my spell. Then a third which I genuinely thought was out. When Dickie gave it not out I said something along the lines of, 'Crikey Dickie you never give me any lb's.'

Dickie replied, 'It were a nip-backer Jim and most o't time they're goin' down. If it 'ad held up, then you'd 'ave had a chance.'

Glancing up at the famous gasometer nearby, I turned to Dickie and said, 'I reckon that if that bloody gasometer was the wicket and I had hit him in front of that, you'd still have given it not out!' Dickie's response was, 'Not unless it 'ad 'eld up!' Much laughter from the non-striker, who I recall was Alan Ealham.

****

Gary Lineker
Tottenham Hotspur, Leicester City AFC and TV sports presenter

When in London, during my days with Tottenham, every September I played cricket for the Cross Arrows at Lords. One Friday, I was talked into bowling. As a batsman, this was against my better judgment.

I duly bowled but managed to tear a muscle in my side. No big deal except that I had a match for Spurs the next day. I made a rather awkward call to Terry Venables who, understandably, was not best pleased. He said he was going to ban me from playing cricket. In the end we compromised and agreed I would never bowl again.

However I dutifully played football the next day. I was in agony and failed to score.

****

Norman McVicker

'Derrick Robbins X1'

I was lucky enough to play for Derrick's team on a number of occasions at Eastbourne - in fact on one I managed a fifty as did 'DHR' in a last wicket stand which pleased him no end!. The matches were all keenly contested but Derrick's hospitality - his X1 being selected from those counties without a fixture on the particular dates - was more than generous to all participating.

We used to stay at The White Friars outside Eastbourne. We would organize collection - and safe return - of a bevy of athletic young ladies from Brighton's Chelsea College to help us through the evening's disco, after a jolly dinner following close of play back at 'The Friars'. (Never did fancy dancing with Norman Graham, the 6'6" tall pace bowler from Kent!)

On one occasion I captained the X1, it being decided we should play three one-day matches, not a straight three-day affair, against Cambridge University. The Undergraduates were perhaps understandably nervous at the dinner, then with the music playing, possibly more so by the presence of nubile young ladies! Unfortunately, we lost the first of the matches but managed a win in the second. Derrick had a word with me prior to the start of the final game saying, 'We're not going to lose this one are we?' 'No way', I replied.

We scored plenty of runs, but bearing in mind DHR's 'briefing' I posted fielders everywhere. Imagine Bob Willis opening the bowling with one slip! He took a hat-trick in the innings. (Prior to departure from Edgbaston I had been instructed by Alan Smith, Warwickshire captain, not to 'over-bowl' him.) However, he managed to 'strain a strut' during his spell, but kept quiet about it when we got back home and negotiated the next county match without hindrance.

Happy days!

****

Colin Beaumont
Yorkshire League wicketkeeper and member of Cleethorpes golf club

'Behind the stumps'

As a wicketkeeper in Yorkshire during the Sixties, one of my roles was to engage opposition batsmen in a little light-hearted banter. On occasion such was not so light-hearted! Anything to disrupt their concentration and aid their speedy return to the pavilion.

During a very tense cup tie, the opposing batsmen had played well and we were delighted to have removed two very good players to put us in a strong position in the match.

At this point out to the wicket strode a young batsman, renowned as a big-hitter but thought not too bright. I had heard he was having to get married to a young lady who was rumoured to be pregnant - or, as it was put to me, had a 'bun' in the oven.

He played a number of deliveries well and, thinking it was time to disturb him a little, I said to him, 'I hear you're getting married soon. Is it a 'bun' job then?'

'Oh no', he replied, 'We're having a three-tiered cake!'

****

R T (Reg) Simpson
Nottinghamshire CCC, England

'Good old George'

During the tour to Australia in 1950/51 on one particular occasion we were flying between two destinations in a Dakota. The crew became acquainted with the fact that I had flown Dakotas as a pilot for nearly 1,200 hours. As a result, they invited me to sit in the First Pilot's seat and asked me to keep an eye on things whilst they went to the back to talk to Denis Compton and others in the party.

Eric Hollies, who hated flying, saw them and asked who was

flying the aircraft. Someone apparently said 'Reg' and he then rushed to the front. The next thing I knew the cabin door was flung open and Eric stood in the entrance with a horrified look on his face. 'What are you doing?' he shouted, and I replied, 'Just keeping an eye on everything.'

Obviously, he did not appreciate the fact that 'George' the automatic pilot, as we called it, was operating and returned to his seat for a stiff whisky! For the remainder of the tour he did his best to avoid flying. I can't recall whether or not he succeeded.

****

Jack Simmons
Lancashire CCC, Chief Executive

'Food glorious food'
Graeme Fowler is aware of my love of food, especially fish and chips. We lived in the same area, as did David Lloyd, and we would often travel in together to Old Trafford.

Returning after a day's play, I asked Graeme to drop me off at my local fish and chip shop which he did. He then added, as it had started to rain, he would run me home and I could eat them there.

He was amazed when I said I preferred to eat them out of the paper and walk home, irrespective of it raining. He replied Jacqueline, my wife, would play hell with him for not dropping me off at the door. We argued a bit about this until I told him the real reason. I wanted to eat them on my way home because if I arrived home with them, she would not make my tea! Hence my appearance as a slightly larger than average player!

****

'Change of name?'
Known as 'flat Jack' because I did not give the ball much flight, tending to fire it in at leg and middle, I returned for pre-season

training after a luxuriant holiday having gained quite a bit of weight!

Clive Lloyd, watching me strip off ready for practice remarked, 'All the journalists will have to abbreviate the flat to fat,' which caused some amusement with the rest of the players.

****

Garry Cook
Abingdon CC

'Sympathy on a cricket field"

I have never subscribed to the view that, on being struck by the ball, one should show no pain. If hit, then I invariably show the discomfort caused. Firstly, it makes me feel better and, secondly, it may encourage the bowler to try more balls I can whack.

Playing against a Reading-based X1, I opened the innings on a quick and bouncy wicket. Early on I popped one up into the vacant short leg area. The opposition responded by assigning a nervous-looking chap to this post close to the bat.

I determined to get rid him of him from there and in advancing to a score of thirty-odd, had already hit one past his ear and another equally hard past his right ankle. By now he looked extremely nervous! I considered one more close call would cause him to retreat. I saw my chance shortly afterwards and launched into a full-blooded pull shot. Sadly the ball was not as short as I thought it was and it came back at me as well, tucking me up and causing a top edge. This slammed into my chin, the seam opening a large cut on my jaw, and dribbled off in the direction of fine-leg. I collapsed in pain, leaking copious amounts of blood onto the pitch and heard my teenage son's voice coming from the pavilion, 'Ha, ha, ha. Dad's down again!' On return from hospital, eight stitches having being required, my captain observed that I had missed out on the run and should have collapsed once I got to the other end!

'Slow play'

Having posted a decent total in a local league match we took the field. The captain of the opposition had an artificial leg and as well as being a good sport and nice chap, he kept wicket very well. (Remarkably well in the circumstances.)

We claimed a couple of early wickets. He came in to bat and proved he could more than handle the bowling and was in for some time. As luck would have it he was struck on his good leg several times, the ball missing all protection and striking flesh. (Our bowling was fairly brisk.) Each time this happened he fell to ground. To our surprise, on each occasion, he ignored the injury to his good leg and proceeded to un-strap and refasten his artificial leg. This took a good few minutes each time, but we made no comment beyond asking if he was OK. Eventually he was out and the innings closed fairly shortly thereafter with a win for us.

After the game I heard the opposing captain remark to our skipper, 'You took a long while to bowl your overs!'

****

'Juniors 1'

Fielding first in a Cherwell League match, our captain gave an early bowl to a 14 year old debutante, Joe Harris, who bowls slow left armers (giving it a huge rip) who at that stage was very short of stature. I was keeping wicket and watched the batsman be comprehensively beaten by all 6 deliveries. It was amazing that none hit the stumps or produced an edge! Changing ends at the end of the over I overhead the lucky batsman remark to his partner ' the best way to play that little b****r is to be at the other end'!

Joe has now grown and played for the various Oxfordshire youth teams.

****

'Juniors 2'

We were playing a friendly all day game in our cricket week and as first change the skipper introduced 13 year old

Samantha to the attack. The batsman, who had been scoring well, promptly played all six deliveries with extreme caution and a maiden ensued. Earwigging again on the change over, I heard him observe to his partner 'there no way I'm getting out to a 13 year old girl'. At the start of Sam's next over the same batsman was facing once again and the first delivery was a poor one – a leg side full toss. Even from behind him you could see the batsman's eyes light up as he went for the big heave. Sadly he got a top edge which gently dollied up to midwicket. This was not the end of it however. At the lunch interval, we were amused to hear that one of the other opposition players had been overhead adding to the batsman's woes by saying 'you know that tour we are going on next week? If you don't want me to tell everybody you got out to a 13 year old girl, you are going to have to buy my drinks all night'.

After lunch, the cricket Gods decided that justice must be done, and when the blackmailer came to the crease he was out for a duck – bowled by Samantha Moore.

Samantha has gone on to play for Oxfordshire Ladies at both junior and senior levels.

****

'A proper shot'

In a league match we had reached a handy 215 for 4 with just over seven overs to go when my son James came to the wicket. He set about the bowling in fine style and early on took the unfortunate bowler from a foot outside off stump for a big six over midwicket. The incensed bowler stared hard at him and shouted 'that wasn't a proper cricket shot!' The next ball was straight, and a bit over pitched, and James lifted it elegantly straight over the centre of the sightscreen for an even bigger six and then enquired of the even more outraged bowler 'was that better?'

At the close of our innings, James had scored 78 not out from 36 balls and put on a hundred with his partner (who had scored twelve of them).

Peter J Graves
Sussex CCC

'The pretty way'
In the Seventies Sussex had a van sponsored by Caffyns. Sussex played Surrey and driving back from the Oval, the van had three occupants: Tony Greig, Peter Graves and Jerry Morley, It was decided by Morley we return home by the 'pretty way' for a change. No motorways!
Graves drove the first stint before giving way to 'Greigy'. The van had one passenger seat and the third passenger sat on the engine cowling between them and in those days vans had sliding doors! With Greig now driving, Morley exclaimed, 'I trust we're going to be safe with you driving Greigy.' 'Don't you worry about a thing Morlers, you have nothing to worry about', replied a confident Greigy who promptly drove into a sharp right-hand bend down a country lane a shade too fast and Morley disappeared out of the open sliding door and into a ditch!

****

'A slippery experience'
Leicestershire v Sussex at Grace Road, circa 1967, 3-day championship match. Leicestershire won the toss and batted in overcast conditions, which after an hour developed into a steady drizzle. John Snow was brought back into the attack for a pre-lunch 'assault' and pleaded to the umpire, Charlie Elliott (then a test umpire) that the ball was like a bar of soap and couldn't the players go off for rain. 'No', replied Charlie.
The luncheon interval saw Peter Marner on 96 not out. The drizzle had not abated and surprisingly at 2.10 pm Sussex again took to the field with Graves and Snow the last to leave the dressing room. I noticed John Snow stuffing a bar of soap inside its wrapping into his pocket. 'You're not going to use that?' I enquired. 'Too bloody right. Elliott makes us start in the rain after the interval and that's not right', replied Snow.

So, first ball after lunch, 'Snowy' ran in to bowl to Marner from the pavilion end and banged in the bar of soap halfway down the pitch. It sat up nicely for Marner who middled it aiming for the gardens over mid-wicket. With everybody looking toward the gardens a 'cloud' of disintegrated soap landed around the wicket area, with a mischievous Mike Griffith picking up a piece and crying 'It tastes like soap!' Peter Marner's face was a picture, Elliott's red with thunder and threatened to report the incident to Lord's.

The match at the time was being covered by Neil Durden-Smith on Radio 2 who unknowingly assumed the delivery was a no ball and that something must have happened to the ball. The upshot over the incident was that 'Snowy' did not face disciplinary action, all the fielders had a real laugh and Peter Marner eventually got his century.

Sadly, those sort of antics on the field don't seem to happen these days..........pity!

****

W (Bob) Taylor MBE, Derbyshire CCC and England

'A bit of a mess'
Touring can be tiring, what with the various grounds, travel, hotels, airports etc and you need a good team spirit throughout. This story relates to the Australia/New Zealand tour of 1974/75.

David Lloyd (Bumble) and Mike Hendrick were 'roomies' and also the jokers of the squad, keen to keep up team spirit. They were often to be found in shops in Australia buying things like stink bombs, exploding cigarettes, Laurel & Hardy face masks etc and playing some very funny tricks on each other.

I recall one particular occasion when we were travelling from Melbourne to Sydney. We were all sitting together awaiting our flight call in the marble-floored departure lounge, when David Lloyd produced a very realistic imitation of a 'dog mess' which he left on the floor just in front of the squad. For the next 15-20 minutes or so, it was hilarious just watching people almost tripping over the thing and generally pulling funny faces.

It was then that we saw hurrying across the lounge a male airport cleaner with his brush and shovel. (Obviously following a complaint by a disgruntled passenger.)

The cleaner was just about to brush this 'mess' onto his shovel when David Lloyd got up, casually picked it up and put it in his pocket. It was absolutely hilarious to see the look on the chap's face! After he realized what had gone on, he had a laugh and joke with us - all good fun to help the tour be a happy one.

****

Joe Blackledge
Former captain, Lancashire CCC

'Language difficulties?'
I remember playing at Hull, and Phil Hough brought a beautiful girl into our hotel. We all said, 'she is a lesbian.' His reply: 'Well, I thought she wasn't English........'

****

Alan Oakman
Sussex CCC, England and Warwickshire CCC

'Pour the tea, Ken'
For fifteen years I shared a room with Ken Suttle when Sussex played away. We would order a pot of tea for two, plus the Telegraph and Mirror for 8am.

If Kenny had been successful the previous day he would always read the Telegraph. If he had a bad day he would read the Mirror!

However, if he had scored a century, or taken a few wickets, he would order tea for two, the Telegraph and Mirror, plus the Times, Mail, Express, Financial Times and any other papers

available, for 7am!
During the fifteen years never once did he pour the tea out - he just read the newspapers!!

****

Alan C ('AC') Smith CBE
Warwickshire CCC and MCC

'Off with the gloves'
I suppose anyone with a long cricket career will have a few embarrassing moments, but not often two in one day.
We were playing Sussex at Hove in midsummer1962 in a typical week-end, three-day match - Saturday, Monday and Tuesday. (There was never any Sunday cricket and I visited friends nearby on the day off.) Returning to the ground on Monday morning I was astonished to see my team-mates out in the field with three substitutes, courtesy of the opposition. Sussex had changed the traditional 11.30am start to 11.00am! Mike Smith and I were both late on parade and David Brown, our fast bowler, had suffered sunstroke.
Later in the day and being a bowler short, I had the rare but welcome chance to cease keeping wicket for a while in order to bowl a little spell. Batting at the time for Sussex was veteran Don Smith, a delightful chap, who had recently returned to the side, I think, from a fractured skull. I was quite sharp in those days and the skipper said, 'No bouncers'.
Endeavouring to follow instructions and pitch the ball up, the first delivery to Don was a head-high 'beamer'. Many apologies. So, too, was the second - profuse apologies and much embarrassment.
6-0-30-0 was a fair return for an ill-controlled spell, but we did win the match!

****

John Spencer
Cambridge 'Blue' and Sussex CCC

'Bouncy, Bouncy!'
It was a sunny August day and Imran Khan was enjoying his first season with Sussex.
There were quite a few top order batsmen in the opposition ranks quite nervous about facing Imran at Hove, traditionally quite green and pacey. Yorkshire were our opponents and I spotted half-a-dozen of their lads looking out at us from the players' viewing gallery as we went through our nets prior to commencement of play.
I went to the wicket and bounced the ball in my hand which came up to my shoulder!
Their openers, Richard Lumb included, came down the stairs and across to the wicket as quick as a flash! Lumb, by now ashen-faced, asked me to bounce the ball again, and was aghast at the extravagant bounce - much to the hilarity of the other Sussex boys, as I had a hard red rubber ball in my hand!

****

Christopher Martin-Jenkins
Cricket Commentator and Cricket Correspondent for 'The Times'

'Extracts from Bedside Cricket'
I know a man who claims to be the only cricketer ever to have scored a hundred before breakfast. He did so in the Sudan where it is rather too hot to play at mid-day!
The same man, Jack Seamer, once played for Somerset at Portsmouth the morning after going to a Commemorative Ball at Oxford. His overnight sleep did not begin until he reached the dressing room at Portsmouth at half-past ten! Two and a half hours later he was woken to be told that Somerset were 40 for five and that, although he had been dropped down the order, he must go in next wicket down. He did so and made his

way slowly to the wicket, his eyes blinking painfully in the unaccustomed brightness.

'Lofty' Herman was bowling for the home side. Jack, a studious and determined player with spectacles and a prominent nose, pushed forward to the first ball which he never saw. He somehow got a touch and edged the ball to third man for a single.. At the other end he played the same stroke towards a slightly slower red blur delivered by Andrew Kennedy, and he vaguely heard a fizzing through the air before the ball thudded into his pads. Frank Chester turned down a thunderous appeal for leg-before. The next ball he actually saw, but as he went back, his studless boots slipped underneath him, and he did a kind of splits. Again ball hit pads; again a loud appeal. This time Chester's finger went up. J W Seamer made his way back to the pavilion, head down, feeling very small and miserable. He gradually became aware that something was making the crowd laugh, but thought nothing of it until he saw the white of the picket fencing before him and looked up to see Herman standing on the square leg boundary.

'Excuse me, mate, he said, pointing towards cover-point, 'but the pavilion is in *that* direction!

****

Concerning Sir Aubrey Smith

Country-house cricket once flourished in Hollywood in the days when C A Smith, the actor and former England cricketer, was playing his permanent role as the archetypal English gentleman. As he grew older, however, Sir Aubrey's eyesight began to fail and to his embarrassment, he dropped a simple catch at slip one day during one of the games over which he would preside with much majesty. Instantly he stopped the game and called for his butler, who walked slowly onto the ground and bowed low. 'Bring me my glasses,' commanded Sir Aubrey.

With due ceremony the butler left the field and returned a few moments later with a pair of spectacles on a silver salver. Sir

Aubrey put them on and signaled to the umpires that they might resume play. The bowler tore in again, refreshed by the break. The batsman pushed timorously forward, edged the ball and watched as Sir Aubrey juggled vainly with the catch and dropped it. Picking up the ball in fury he yelled across to the watching butler: 'Hetherington, you idiot, you brought my *reading* glasses!'

****

'Anon'
Village Cricket
On a hot afternoon a member of the visiting side having bowled fourteen overs in sweltering heat and after consuming the tea-time sandwiches and cakes, went for a drink at the pub adjoining the ground. He must have been thirsty for he consumed four or five pints of local cider. He tottered back to the ground to find his team in trouble needing five runs to win with seven wickets down. As a natural number eleven, he began putting his pads on in anticipation of a visit to the crease to help his side to victory. By this time he was in a real state! His captain, meeting him at the crease told George three runs were needed to win the match. George replied he was seeing three of everything and the captain suggested that if that was the case, he should aim for the middle ball. He did, missed and was bowled. Game lost! On the way back to the pavilion the captain berated poor George for not playing at the middle of the three balls as instructed. George's short reply was he played the middle ball with the wrong bat!

****

J M (Mike) Brearley OBE
Cambridge University, Middlesex CCC and England
captain

Tribute to M J Smith, Middlesex CCC and England

Four years ago my colleague, and for several years opening batting partner at Middlesex, Mike Smith, died suddenly of a heart attack at his home in Enfield. I had known Mike since we were both seventeen, when he was captain of the Middlesex Young Amateurs. I remember him then as a powerful striker of the ball, playing strokes I could only dream of, like hitting fast bowlers past mid-on with a straight bat.

Beginning his career as a left arm spinner, he became a fine attacking batsman for his county and was unlucky not to earn more than four caps in one-day international matches.

I remember several shared experiences, not least his courage and humour, both of which were evident in annual tussles with John Snow at Hove on Bank Holidays in August. They were like a preview or sideshow to the match itself. Lively pitches, sea air, a decent smattering of spectators and then the hostile but amusing barrage from 'Snowy' to be met with an array of hooks, pulls, near misses, dropped catches, sixes, fours, and then sanity returned. Mike ('Smudge') getting out and the game proper starting again. Mike would often get Middlesex off to a racing start!

I recall he ran me out for a duck at Lord's against Lancashire. This was the ace of trumps of run-outs! I came in at number three and Mike was facing either Peter Lever or Ken Shuttleworth. I had not faced a ball when 'Smudge' pushed a 'no-ball' delivery wide of mid-on and called me for a run. I thought it must be an easy single but I was run out by a good yard! Run out off a no-ball and without facing a ball! I had to leave the wicket, passing Mike on my way back to the pavilion. I was probably the only one not to see the humour of it.

I recall an excellent occasion at the Oval, when we scored 400 plus on the first day. Geoff Arnold bowled the first over of the match. He was a marvelous bowler with the new ball, able to bowl brisk away swingers, so late in their movement that you were not sure whether they moved in the air or off the pitch. The first five balls pitched on off-stump and moved away, passing Mike's outside edge. (Surrey were never slow to voice their complaints when things went against them and the Middlesex players, watching from the balcony, were mixed in their emotions as much about the deviation as the complaining of the Surrey players!) The sixth delivery was a no-ball which swung the other way and going through the 'gate' clipped the top of leg stump and flew to fine leg for four byes. The seventh ball Mike smashed through the covers for four. The sheer injustice of this - Middlesex 8-0 after one over - was a delight.

In the early '70s I had some uncertain and unhappy times. I was quite miserable and unsure of myself. More than once I nearly resigned. Throughout Mike was a pillar of support. He was extremely generous and loyal. He always stood by me and encouraged me. As vice-captain or senior player, his advice was of a particular kind. He would often offer a long view, thoughtful and prescient. I came to realize that he and Clive Radley complimented each other perfectly. Mike offered the detached view, Clive always down to earth and immediate. Both were generous in that they would not take offence if I did not follow their suggestions.

Then in the late '70s or early '80s when it came to issues of team selection and his place was no longer so certain - a time that is really hard for sportsmen - he had no illusions and was never bitter or envious about players who replaced him in the team.

He took on captaincy of the second X1 to bring on our young players and did a marvelous job in that role.

Subsequently, Mike became Middlesex scorer for ten years, following in the footsteps of two other great characters of Middlesex cricket, Jim Sims and Harry Sharp, a role which enabled him to offer to another generation his shrewdness, knowledge, generosity, humour and warmth.

****

Revd Andrew Wingfield Digby
Oxford University and ordained Church minister

To my - and my family's - utter amazement I was selected to play for Oxford University in their first match of the season against Warwickshire in The Parks. A certain Norman McVicker came in as night watchman on the first evening and early the next morning he succumbed to my innocuous bowling, thus providing me with my very first 'first class' wicket. I honestly cannot remember how he was out but am sure his story of being caught on the boundary is fictitious! The next man in was MJK Smith.

My eccentric cousin, who knew how bad I was as a bowler, bet me two bottles of champagne that I would not get the great man out. I clean bowled him for two with a cleverly dipping half volley that he missed! My cousin leapt from his deck chair whooping and hollering. He comprised about half the crowd and disturbed the other half so much that it started barking.

I never got the champagne!

****

'Anon'

'Memories'

When we were young, we couldn't wait for net practice nights, mingling and learning from the older, senior, players - who would always spare a word of encouragement to those keen to learn - just basically bowling to them, retrieving balls from the outfield and then, perhaps, getting your pads on for a few deliveries in fading light! On match days, helping the scorer by maintaining the scoreboard and hoping for a 'free' tea for your efforts.

During nets, the selection committee would meet every Monday in the pavilion to choose next week-end's teams. When young and aspiring, you would admire the names on the team sheet and hope one day your name might appear on the lists.

Later, when we did appear, entering the changing room for the very first time on a match day was daunting, but the seniors and others made you welcome, understanding your nervousness.

We all had our good days and bad days as we progressed, hopefully, through the 3rd's, 2nd's to the 'glory' of the 1st X1. We enjoyed the game, at whatever level, and all the 'ups' and 'downs'. (Probably more 'downs' than 'ups'!)

Now where are we? Lounging around the boundary in deck-chairs or standing adjacent to the bar with a beer in our hand - and perhaps a bit of a paunch - easily commenting on what is going on in the match: "He's no spin bowler. Why is that man still at point? No third slip! Should get the opening bowler back on. What! He won the toss and put them in......." etc.

We old players should be encouraging the young players, as I am sure we do in our own way and I am reticent to criticise any player, because I remember very well the words of an old North American Indian saying: *"Let me not criticise my neighbour until I have walked ten miles in his moccasins."*

Perhaps worth remembering in our dotage ....

****

Bryan Richardson
Warwickshire CCC, former chairman Coventry City FC

"Only the English and only at Lord's"

A number of years ago I was at Lord's during a Test match standing in front of the Tavern. A chap whom I vaguely knew through club cricket came up and started about the match. All of a sudden he said:

"You knew Commander Mike Aynsworth?"

"Yes - I played against him when he opened the batting for the Combined Services."

"Poor chap died last week - playing cricket."

"How sad", I said, "At least he died doing what he loved most -

playing cricket."
"Very strange though", he replied.
"Why?" I asked.
"He died fielding in the gully and he'd always fielded at slip!"

****

John Lever MBE
Essex CCC and England

'Fun in the Sun'
With the changes in the professional game demanding greater fitness and, some say, more dedication, it is easy to see that some of the fun may have gone from the first class game. Whilst basically the same sport, improved financial rewards have created additional pressure.

Thankfully, this was not the case many years ago when Essex opened their programme with a visit to Fenners. It was the same year David Lloyd started his career as a first class umpire. He was slightly apprehensive, given the Essex reputation for antics on the field and had the added pressure of being watched by Doug Insole, chairman of the umpire's committee.

A plea from David for a quiet game naturally fell on deaf ears. He threw me the new ball to get the match under way and as I marched back to my mark, swapped it for a ball which had seen at least 200 overs. The batsman played forward and pushed the tatty bit of leather back down the pitch. I picked the ball up and asked David if he thought the ball had gone out of shape. There was a look of horror on his face, followed by much chuckling from the rest of the team, then turning into a smile as the real new ball was produced from mid-off.

Further pleas from David asking us to behave were listened to and the apology beers were bought that night!

I do wonder if a report or a fine would have followed in today's game. One would hope not! Enjoy your cricket but enjoy the GAME more!!

****

Graham Gooch
Essex CCC and England captain

'One of my favourites'
Jack Van Geloven, a pleasant, if rather strict Yorkshireman
who used to play for Leicestershire, later became a first class
umpire. At Tunbridge Wells, against Kent, last ball before
lunch, Ray East is caught at mid-wicket, the fielder diving and
just scooping it up. Ray thinks it's a bump-ball so he just stands
there. Van Geloven has a little think and then up comes his
finger, 'Out'. On the way in for lunch Ray walks in with Jack,
saying, "Okay I'm off Jack but I could swear it was a bump-
ball."
"Get away, lad, that was a fair catch. You're out", was the
reply.
All through lunch, as we were sitting there, Ray is still rucking
on that he wasn't out and it was a bump-ball. Jack sits there
enjoying his tuck and thinking quietly, "I dunno what's the
world coming to? East was out and that's all there is to it."
So the bell goes. Out go the umpires, out go Kent. East is in the
dressing room, putting on a different coloured helmet, different
gloves and carrying a different bat. And out he goes again. Van
Geloven had no idea, of course.
Ray is at Jack's end and just as the bowler was about to deliver
the first ball after lunch, East turns his new helmet to Van
Geloven, looks him straight in the eye and says, "You did say
that was a bump-ball, didn't you, Jack?" Van Geloven leapt out
his skin and nearly collapsed on the spot!

****

People like Van Geloven, the veterans who have seen it all and
done it all as players, are like old and firm friends, sort of
uncles in charge on the beach. Remember old Arthur Jepson of
Nottinghamshire? 'Dusty' Miller comes in to bat: "Mornin'

Arthur."

"Mornin' Dusty lad, did you use the motorway this morning...?" or, "I've a gippy tummy after that breakfast she gave me". That sort of general and friendly chat. So this time, when Arthur says, "You'll have no trouble on this pitch, Dusty lad, the others don't seem to realise it. All you've got to do is get right forward everytime and this bowling's a heap of crap." Right, thinks Miller, nice nod and a wink there from old Jeppo, thanks very much.

So, next over, Dusty is facing and Arthur at the bowler's end. First ball he plays the most extravagant forward defensive of all time, right down the track with a long left leg, just like Arthur had said. The ball hits him in the middle of the pad. Big appeal.

Finger up. "That's plumb, lad, sorry!" said Jepson as he sent him on his way.

****

D W (Dave) Marshall
Ross Group Sports Club

'A memory of Colin Milburn. Northants CCC, England'

Ross Group hosted a benefit match for that fine Northants and England wicketkeeper, Keith Andrew, during the mid-sixties. Keith had arranged for a goodly number of his colleagues to attend, including Colin Milburn, 'reinforced' by a number of players from the Yorkshire side they were playing at Headingly in a championship match.

Ross fielded our 1stX1 from the Lincolnshire League. Northants won the toss and asked us to take first knock. I recall we posted a reasonable total.

Northants began their reply with Colin taking to the crease - I'm afraid I cannot recall his fellow opener - to thunderous applause from the large crowd gathered to see their favourites. After a few overs with Colin leading the way, he faced my bowling for the first time. He nicked my outswinger and was caught behind by the Ross 'keeper, Alan Borman. I appealed and up went the umpire's finger. What a scalp! A bit of 'David and Goliath!!'

I received a bit of applause, plus a few boos, on his return to the pavilion.

After the game, chatting at the bar with him (he was one of my heroes), I said I was sorry I had appealed, because in recent weeks he had been smashing 4's and 6's from assorted county attacks without any let up and the crowd had been looking forward to more of the same stuff on the day.

He seemed to tower over me - he was a large man, to say the least - as he replied, 'Never mind, David, it was a good ball and you did me a favour, as I needed a bit of a rest after the exertions of the past few weeks!'

What a great leveller cricket is. Me on top of the world and Colin well rested! What a wonderful game.

****

Alan Barnsley
Crusaders CC

Although I was a very lowly local player, I've always been an avid and enthusiastic supporter of cricket. My most memorable cricketing moment was, however, not at a cricket match but at a wedding!

A close friend of our family married Kevin Jarvis, at that time an excellent fast bowler for Kent, in a team containing stars like Mark Benson, Alan Knott, Derek Underwood, Mike Denness, Mark Ealham, Chris Cowdrey, etc. My wife, Jenny, and I were invited to the wedding and our four year old son, Mark, was a page boy with Alan Knott's son. The wedding, at Sandwich, was attended by many of the Kent players.

There was I amongst the stars of Kent! It was quite awe inspiring but contrary to my perceived expectation, they were all so very approachable, pleasant and down to earth - real people!

To meet so many stars and feel relaxed in their company has lived with me ever since.

****

Ron Gardner
Treasurer, Lincolnshire Cricket Lovers' Society

'Memories of wartime Bradford'
The early years of the second world war were an exciting time for an eleven year old schoolboy in Bradford.

In winter there were Saturday afternoons at Park Avenue, where we were thrilled by such soccer stars as Len Shackleton, Stanley Matthews and Sam Bartram. At Odsall, there was the fine Rugby League team, Bradford Northern and for the musically inclined, the Halle Orchestra conducted by the great Sir John Barbirolli.

The highlight for me, however, was the cricket season. I was lucky enough to live within half a mile of Bowling Old Lane Cricket Ground - one of the teams of the Bradford League. Saturday for us youngsters consisted of playing for our school team in the morning and then, after a quick bite of dinner, dashing to play in the Bradford League (usually in the second team) against the same players with whom we had played at school in the morning.

Naturally, being so close to the ground, all my spare time was spent there. As had happened in the first world war, many great players graced the Bradford League - including Learie Constantine, Bill Copson, Tommy Mitchell, Eddie Paynter, Winston Place and occasionally, Len Hutton. The star attraction was Learie Constantine who could fill the grounds to capacity with spectators

At Bowling Old Lane, we had as our professional Arthur Booth who topped the first class averages immediately after the war. Illustrious members of the first eleven (while I was stuck in the second team) were Frank Lowson and Bob Appleyard who both went on to gain international honours.

Our president was Mr Ernest Holdsworth, who was also chairman of the Yorkshire County Club and who, on one memorable occasion, invited the great George Hirst for an evening's coaching with the young boys. I still well remember what a kind, courteous gentleman he was. When Arthur Mitchell came on another occasion, that was indeed a very different kettle of fish!

These are still treasured memories and I hope that today's teenagers get as much enjoyment from cricket as I did as a young schoolboy growing up in Bradford.

****

Norman McVicker

Many years ago, when Ivan Madray was club professional at Ross Group, a benefit match for him was staged at the now defunct Ross sports ground. The West Indies were on tour and, generously, on their day off during a three-day match at Scarborough, agreed to turn out for the occasion. They came in strength in Ivan's support. We were blessed by a sunny day and a good attendance and good cricket.

My brother-in-law Garry, then only a youngster, volunteered to help with the scoreboard on the day, entitling him to a free tea during the interval between innings. He was clearly in awe of the occasion, sitting eating his tea in the company of such legendary cricketers such as Wes Hall, Rohan Kanhai, Lance Gibbs, Seymour Nurse, Basil Butcher, Joe Solomon and so on.

The match was a foregone conclusion of course, Ivan's side being well beaten, but it was an entertaining afternoon's cricket with world stars on parade. Giving Garry a lift back home after the game, he piped up from the back seat he had had a marvellous time and that Mr (Wes) Hall had spoken to him during the tea interval. 'That's good', I said. 'What did he say to you?' His wide-eyed reply was, 'Please pass me the jam, son.'

****

Yvonne Fairchild
Bornemouth

'A Devonian dilemma'
Once upon a time there were two farmers named George and
Fred. Their farms were situated relatively close together across
their respective fields and joined by a country lane.
George owned a young sow (a gilt) called Wilhemina who
came to the age where George felt it was time to mate her and
acquire for his farm a litter of little piglets.
Knowing that Fred owned a pig, George rang his friend and
suggested that he should mate his sow with Fred's pig.
Fred readily agreed and said that as they were friends he would
charge George a fee of only £5.00.
George was happy with this and said that they lived so close he
would pop Wilhemina into his wheelbarrow and bring her
down the lane to Fred's farm that very afternoon.
This he did, the pig and sow were put together in the pen and
over a cup of tea, Fred told George to look for the signs of a
successful mating next morning. 'Remember, if she's lying
down in the straw first thing, we haven't been successful, but if
she's standing up eating grass we're in business,' he said.
George took Wilhemina home in the wheelbarrow and next
morning woke early to check on her condition. He could see
the pig pen from his bedroom window, so just had to draw
back the curtains and look out. Unfortunately, Wilhemina was
lying down in the straw and so was not pregnant.
George decided to have another try and rang Fred to ask if he
could bring Wilhemina to his pig for a second try. George said,
'No problem, but I'm afraid I'll have to ask you for another
£5.00. 'That's all right George,' replied Fred, 'You're giving me
a very good rate anyway. 'I'll just put her in the wheelbarrow
and bring her down again this afternoon.'
So he duly placed Wilhemina in the wheelbarrow and wheeled
her down the lane to Fred's farm.
The same procedure was followed, with the same reminder,
'Don't forget if she's lying down in the straw, bad news. If she's

standing up eating grass, you're on!'

Next morning George leapt out of bed and drew back the curtains to check the pig pen. Once again Wilhemina was lying in the straw.

George was so disappointed but decided it could be 'third time lucky', so rang Fred yet again to make an appointment. Fred was quite happy but said he would have to charge another £5.00. George felt it would be worth the outlay to have a fine litter of pigs, so agreed.

Wilhemina was put in the wheelbarrow once again and wheeled to Fred's farm.

Next morning George awoke with Wilhemina on his mind and said to his wife, 'I can't bear to look. You look out and tell me what she's doing.'

George's wife drew back the curtains and George said, 'Well, is she lying down in the straw?' His wife replied, 'No, she's not lying down in the straw.' George, brightening, said, 'Is she standing up eating grass?' His wife responded, 'No, she's not standing up eating grass.' George, now more than curious, said, 'Well what IS she doing?'

'Well,' said his wife, ' she's sitting in the wheelbarrow!'

****

Salford Economists

This team from the University was comprised of lecturers and played friendly matches whenever they could. On one occasion a player gave two colleagues a lift home after the game. The following morning he discovered a £10 note in his car.

Clearly the money did not belong to him, so he telephoned the first of his colleagues to enquire if he might have dropped it inadvertently. After a few seconds , back came the answer, 'No, not mine'. He then telephoned the second, who happened to be treasurer for the team, and after a minute or so, having looked in his wallet and elsewhere, responded, 'Yes, I think it might well be mine' and proceeded to reel off the serial number of the missing note. Spot on! Wow, what a treasurer!

****

Geoff Miller
Derbyshire and Essex CCC, England

'Room mates on tour.'
The modern era of cricket tours allows each individual a room
by himself. Therefore wives and families are relaxed in their
husbands' company.
So different from my days of touring. I roomed with snorers,
eccentrics, routine freaks, and mirror practisers, and ...... Derek
Randall (!?!)
Bernard Thomas, the physio, was the roomy coordinator.
Suffice to say, he took a lot of flak.
'Arkle' (Derek Randall) would run a bath, nip next door in only
a towel to borrow some shampoo and inadvertently lock
himself out, necessitating a journey down to reception for a
spare key.
Many was the time when one of us had to phone down to room
service for another cup as he had 'juggled' one onto the floor!!
Chris Tavare, a lovely bloke, would make a morning cup of tea
.... at 6am! Fine if I got to bed at 9 pm. Not so good if it was
nearer 1 am.
He had to be told!!
Ian Botham and Alan Lamb were interesting?? Alan Knott had
to do his 100 sit ups (with the windows closed .... no draughts,
stiff neck!!!)
Never got to room with Geoff Boycott. Come to think of it,
never roomed on the same floor as him! Bowled a lot at him
though.
I went on six England tours and enjoyed every minute of them
all. Meeting and getting used to rooming with so many
different characters was fascinating. Long life friendships have
ensued.
John Lever, Graham Gooch, Peter Willey, Ian Botham, John

Emburey and many more have become really good friends.

I look back with fondness to my father who told me, as a teenager, passionate about the game of cricket, 'If you are lucky enough to make the grade as a professional cricketer, the way of life is just as important as the way you play.'

He also said, you have only to turn one ball to put doubt in the batsman's mind...........

If only I could have turned that one ball I am sure the game would have been much easier.

Chris Tarrant
TV Presenter and member of The Lord's Taverners

One of the nice things about summer is playing cricket with the Lord's Taverners. The Taverners are a motley collection of actors, disc jockeys, film stars, comedians and hardened criminals that hold very well organized and highly entertaining sporting get-togethers all over Britain to raise money for charity. They invariably make thousands of pounds for the charities concerned and lots of very famous people give up their spare time to come and help. When they are really struggling they ring people like me instead to make up the numbers.

One of the nicest ones I did was at a large Midlands cricket club a couple of years ago. All sorts of famous stars had turned up. The sun shone, the champagne flowed, and it was a delightful Sunday afternoon. The Taverners were fielding, telling each other jokes and passing round hip flasks, and one particular section of the crowd who had not seen much of the match - as they had been stuck solid in the beer tent since eleven in the morning - were becoming noticeably more noisy as the match progressed. They seemed to be mainly long-haired motor-cyclists with motifs like 'Motorhead are Magic' and 'I could eat Meatloaf' written across their chests and eventually, it had to happen: on comes a streaker to huge guffaws of laughter and wild applause. The long, black hair flowing over his naked, tattooed shoulders, the defiant figure came roaring on to the middle of that sacred turf, the clenched fist raised to acknowledge the salute of the crowd not wearing a single stitch.

Now the problem streakers normally have is how to finish their act. It's always an absolute show-stopper greeted with wild, abandoned applause and then before he ever needs to do anything else the police appear and remind him why they are always kitted out with pointed hats. Struggling and protesting, the helmet covering the dangly bits, off goes the streaker applauded all the way. But, this being a Taverners affair, and the Taverners being the sort of hardened worldly-wise people that they are, nobody can actually give a monkeys. The police stand beaming benevolently, arms folded, from the front of the happy crowd and we say things like 'Go on, do something now you're here' or 'Are you seriously going to take that back to your girlfriend?' The defiant hero out in the middle of the pitch becomes noticeably less defiant as the seconds tick by and the deafening cheers of the crowd turn first to embarrassed giggles and then to callous catcalls and slights on his manhood.

I don't know how far it is from the middle of a cricket pitch to the boundary, but it must have been the longest walk that poor bloke ever took in his life and to this day I still wonder if he ever got his clothes back.

****

Alan Lamb
Hampshire CCC and England

A very amusing tale happened in Calcutta, India in the early 1980's. The game was about to start and England were bowling with Ian (Beefy) Botham taking the new ball. Beefy started running in to deliver the first ball of the day but failed to release the ball and carried on running towards the pavilion. We all looked at each other and started to laugh as we knew he had a problem and was dashing to the toilet in a serious panic. Having seen very unpleasant marks of the back of his trousers, we realized he had not made it in time.

Ten minutes had passed and the Indian crowd were getting restless and were chanting for Ian Botham. So before a riot started, our manager went into the dressing room toilets and asked Beefy if we could have the ball back as Beefy has taken the ball with him and there was going to be a riot if play did not start.

****

Bryan Swift
Grimsby Town CC and Lincolnshire CCC

'The missing scorer'
I can still laugh when thinking of the 'Yorkshire Council' years and, in particular, a game at Rotherham.
Harry Abe, the Town scorer, enjoyed a drink and social gatherings. After the game the wine was flowing and later in the evening we gathered in the coach. I believe 'Twigs' Wilson counted all on board and off we went in the direction of Doncaster. For reasons not quite clear, somebody remarked that Harry was missing, even though all seats were taken! The reason for this was that one of the opposition players lived in Doncaster and had begged a lift home.
We, therefore, had to return to the cricket ground and there was Harry, face all aglow, enjoying his evening with the members. Needless to say some folk were not exactly happy at their late arrival home!

****

Tom Graveney OBE
Gloucestershire, Worcestershire CCC and England

In 1966 I lived in a small town just outside Cheltenham on what was the A46 then. The house was on the main road and on Sundays I used to clean up the front of the house.
I had just got back into the Test team on my 39th birthday and

done well against the West Indies.

Anyhow I was doing my Sunday chore, when a couple of youngsters cycled by. The bigger of the two turned to his friend and said, 'Hey, Tom Graveney lives there.' The little fellow said, 'Go on, whereabouts?' His friend replied, 'Where that old fellow is sweeping up.'

****

Philip Sharpe
Yorkshire and Derbyshire CCC, England

One of my favourite recollections is from the early '60's concerning a Yorkshire match against Gloucestershire at Bristol. There was always considerable rivalry between Brian Close and I as to who would take the most catches during a season. This particular year we were neck and neck.

In the middle of the afternoon, on a very pleasant day, Ray Illingworth was bowling to Martin Young from the pavilion end, turning the ball up the slope of course and not a happy 'bunny'. Closey was at short leg about 45 degrees and me in my customary position at slip. Martin put 'the lap' on Illy from outside off stump, connected quite well and it smacked Closey, who was still crouching, smack on the forehead and rebounded to me at slip high up to my left which I caught, thereby claiming the catch.

(From the boundary it must have looked as if he had headed the ball across to me for which I thanked him profusely.)

Obviously there was a great deal of laughter around, even the outgoing batsman had to smile but was there any, 'Well caught, 'Sharpey' or something of that ilk from the captain? I'm afraid not. Only, 'Well you jammy, cheating p.......', or something similar. 'You are even pinching my bloody catches now!'

****

Trevor E Bailey OBE
Cambridge University, Essex CCC and England

'Memories of D C S Compton'
One stroke which will always be associated with Denis Compton was the sweep which he played later than most and made sure of keeping the ball on the ground, because his bat was sloping down at the moment of contact. The golden summer for the 'golden boy' was 1947, when he scored more runs and more centuries than anybody in the history of the game. At the end of that season I found myself batting with Denis against the South Africans in the Hastings Festival. A vast crowd had turned up in the hope of seeing him complete yet another record. My fear was that I would run him out, which seemed the only way he could be dismissed - and was by no means improbable, as his calling was wonderfully unpredictable. On this occasion the calamity was avoided. He not only made batting look easy, he made it look fun.
One way to score very fast is to give the strike to a player like Flintoff, by stealing a single off the first ball of every over and never taking one off the last when you had strike. I joined Denis after he had already completed a very flamboyant century against Pakistan at Trent Bridge and we then put on 192 in about 100 minutes with some 90% of the runs flowing from his mercurial bat. He was more than a great player, he was essentially an entertainer.

****

Jeff Todd
Heywood, Cleethorpes CC

'First team debut'
Being selected as a young lad of sixteen in the first team you have played as a youngster is a daunting prospect.
However, as I entered the changing rooms, three or four of the senior players were present and the skipper introduced me to

the others.

I chose a peg to start to get changed. However, I was immediately told Ralph Farmer changes there. I moved to the other side only to be told Jack Wilson changes there. After a third move - and being told that was Ray Flaherty's peg - I eventually got changed on a little peg in the corner out of the way.

So much for making me relaxed and feel welcome!

****

'No return, Andy'

North Marine Road, at Scarborough, provided the setting for a match with Cleethorpes. Scarborough were batting and coming to the end of their innings. Fifty overs showed on the scoreboard and Keith Phillips, the Cleethorpes captain, sent Andy down to fine leg in front of the pavilion for the final over.

However Andy, who hated fielding, thought the innings was completed and the skipper was sending him off to freshen up before opening the innings. Andy left the pitch and went off to the changing rooms to get ready.

After two or three minutes, when no one else has entered the changing rooms, Andy went to the door and saw the final over being bowled. When he tried to get back on the field the umpires refused and he had to wait until the team came off when he received a severe ticking off from the skipper.

As it was we didn't need him in that last over - but we all had a laugh with a drink in the bar afterwards.

****

Derek L Underwood MBE
Kent CCC and England

'The rewards of hanging on in there as night-watchman'
Having fended off the bowling of Dennis Lillee for twenty minutes in a Sydney Test match in my role as night-watchman, I was pleased to return to the dressing room in one piece. I was not too enamoured when Dennis Lillee, who had been calling me all the names under the sun, came into the England dressing room and thrust a can of beer into my hand. I turned to him and said, 'Give me ten minutes and I'll join you for a beer then you two-faced ....' (I always needed half-an-hour to unwind from the job of night-watchman.) As always a few beers were drunk and some fun had by all, with us leaving the ground in darkness.
Iam Botham turned to me that evening and said, 'If you bat out the session until lunch tomorrow, I'll treat you to a case of beer.'
The morning session went quite well, with a few runs off the edge, and the occasional semi-drive or push. I had quite long partnerships with Mike Brearley and Derek Randall and guess what? I was still there an hour and a half later. I made it through to lunch and 42 not out! The boys gave me a great reception when I walked into the dressing room and yes, there was Botham with a cigarette for me and, where I was changing, a case of beer.
Both said, 'There you are Deadly, 24 cans of Tooheys.' Rest day tomorrow. You deserve them. Guess what. Twenty-four cans later, Both had had eighteen of them and I had six! I enjoyed them especially as they were on him.
By the way, when he batted he made a duck!

****

Allan Knott
Kent CCC and England

'Conned'
During the 1981 5th Test v Australia at Old Trafford, Ian Botham really conned me. I had just caught Martin Kent, cutting at John Emburey. As Dennis Lillee came out to bat, Alan Curtis, who for years had done the tannoy for Tests, made an announcement which I didn't hear. I asked Ian about it and when he said it referred to some sort of record for Dennis Lillee, I started clapping. Then Ian revealed: 'You've just obtained the record for wicket-keeping victims against Australia.' A voice from the crowd shouted, 'Stop showing off, Knott', because I was clapping myself. Ian Botham had really caught me out!

****

James Edward Cook
Abingdon CC

'Vale'
When my grandfather was a young man he was a more than useful and keen cricketer, playing for local village clubs, before joining Louth and subsequently Grimsby Town. (He could not have been too bad a player, managing the 'double' one season!)
He became friendly with a certain Captain Webb, himself a former cricketer, who from the boundary spotted some potential in Ted Cook's ability, and as he had connections with Nottinghamshire CCC suggested he could arrange a trial at Trent Bridge if he was interested..
Grandad was farming in Yarborough at the time, working hard - as all farmers seemed to do in those days - and was unable to accept the invitation and, eventually, as years went by they lost contact. Grandad continued to farm and played whenever he could, which seemed to be often, before donning the white coat

for a number of years.

Quite some years later it was decided my father, when he was two years old, should have his tonsils removed. Apparently, before the operation he kicked up such a fuss in the ward he was moved to a side room, where he continued as a major disruption to a normally more peaceful Louth hospital routine.

In the next room was an old man, desperately ill, who asked of the nursing staff who was making such a racket. 'Oh, it's Ted Cook's son', was the reply. The old gentleman thought for a minute then responded, 'I used to know a Ted Cook once, years ago. When he next comes to the hospital, would you ask him if he can spare a minute?'

Accordingly, when grandad next visited he did go in to see the old gentleman and was astonished to find the patient was none other than Captain Webb. It must have been a touching moment for both men and, sadly, Captain Webb died two days later.

****

H D (Dickie) Bird
Yorkshire and Leicestershire CCC, Test umpire

'A natural calling'
During a Test match - England v West Indies - I urgently needed to use the toilet, so I stopped the match and said to the players, 'I am sorry gentlemen but nature calls,' and off I sped to the changing rooms much to the amusement of the players and a tremendous roar from the crowd.

****

'A mystery?'
After a match at Northampton - Northants v Somerset - I went to the car park but to my absolute amazement someone had taken off the wheels of my car and they were resting against the railings.

On my windscreen there was a note which read, 'All the very best Dickie, have a good journey home.' I always wonder if it was Allan Lamb and Ian Botham who were responsible for the prank....

(Editor's note.) 'Dickie' Bird after scoring 181 not out for Yorkshire v Glamorgan in 1959, was left out of the side for the following match and never played for Yorkshire again!

****

Barbara Dickson
Singer and actress

We have a great friend, the best man at our wedding and my husband's oldest friend from school.
He was at one stage a professional cricket for Middlesex and Gloucestershire in the 1980's.
His wife Brenda called the ground one day and asked to speak to him, to be told he had just gone in to bat.
'It's all right', she replied, 'I'll just hold!'

****

Sir Ian Botham
Somerset, Worcestershire and Durham CCC, England

During my years at Somerset in the late 70's and 80's I actually lived not too far from Cleethorpes in Epworth! In the early days of my career my winter employment was with my father-in-law's business in Thorne, and therefore Kath and I decided to live in the North. The days at home with Kath, Liam, and Sarah were very precious, and few and far between, especially when my England call-up came and Winter tours became part of the agenda.
As I became more well-known, going places with the family became more and more difficult and Kath was often walking

ahead, either with toddler Liam or baby Sarah, unaware of the fact I had been waylaid by some cricketing enthusiasts.

We had, at times, to escape this and where did we go? Cleethorpes, with its miles of sand and the occasional glimpse of water - first one to see the sea gets a sixpence! Whilst Liam and Sarah loved the freedom of running along in their little red wellies with the boxer dogs along, Mum and Dad had time to relax and enjoy being a family. We had lots of laughs on those outings and invariably ended up back in Epworth with a boot full of sand, soggy dogs and two very tired, but happy, children.

****

Arthur Fairchild, Member, Middlesex CCC

Scene - Naval Transit Camp, Ceylon 1946, after the war with Japan.

Naval staff were responsible for the welfare of some 3,000 personnel en-route to UK and demobilisation.

One Naval man was responsible for typing and distributing 'Orders of the Day' to all parts of the camp. The heading of these instructions was always the same:

ORDERS OF THE DAY
REVEILLE 6.30 AM
DRESS OF THE DAY - TROPICAL GEAR
OPTIONAL SHIRTS

There followed a detailed list of sporting activities designed to keep the ratings happy. On one particular day the Commanding Officer telephoned the typist to point out that the letter 'R' was missing from the word SHIRTS.

This led to the unfortunate typist being asked if a certain bodily function was always compulsory!!

****

Howard Swain
Cleethorpes CC

'Pitch 'em up'

When Cleethorpes were admitted to the Yorkshire League in the 1980's, it was the first time a club outside the county became a member. It also meant our 2nd X1 playing in the Ridings League against all the other second elevens of the Yorkshire League sides.

I was 43 at the time, but still opening the bowling for the 2nd X1. This new venture for our club came a little late in my cricketing career, but it enabled me to play on First Class grounds of the time, namely Scarborough, Harrogate, Bradford, Sheffield Collegiate and Hull, although the latter was past its best by then.

As the years progressed, I became a change bowler, giving up-and-coming bowlers a chance to shine. In one particular game they were being hit to all parts of the ground, mainly due to their lack of line and length. In fact, for some reason, they were consistently bowling so short that the mid-wicket and square-cover boundaries were seeing too much of the ball as the batsmen showed how strong they were off the back foot.

Enter yours truly as captain Roy Oslear threw me the ball and said, 'For goodness sake, Howard, pitch the bloody ball up!'

Always one to obey the captain's instructions, I duly obliged. The expression on Roy's face became a sight to behold as the batsman immediately drove my first ball back over my head for six. After a stunned silence, I turned to Roy saying, 'Did I pitch it up far enough skipper?'

****

Ray Illingworth CBE
Yorkshire, Leicestershire CCC, England

A true story that happened when I was captain of England during the Test match v West Indies at Edgbaston during the '73 series.

I arrived on the ground well over an hour and a quarter before play was due to start on the Saturday to find Arthur Fagg, the umpire, was refusing to stand because he had been having trouble with the West Indies' team not accepting his decisions.

I tried to contact officials at Lord's but it was Saturday and nobody was working. I then tried to contact the chairman of selectors, Alec Bedser, or any of the selectors, but they were all out on the Edgbaston golf course - so it was all down to me.

After talking to Arthur for about an hour, I eventually managed to persuade him to let Alan Oakman stand for the first over of the day's play and then come on and take over himself, his protest having been made.

The match was due to start and I still hadn't had time to change into my whites! I occasionally allow myself these days when I see the set-up (even the helpers have helpers) to ponder how the game has changed.

****

Rosemary McVicker
(Long-suffering wife of Norman)

My husband had attracted a small group of young 'fans' at various Sussex grounds and whenever Warwickshire/Leicestershire appeared, the girls were in attendance. They also kept in touch with him with birthday/Christmas cards during the winter months and the occasional letter.

1976 - a very dry summer as I recall - Leicestershire visited Eastbourne and I made the trip in company of two good friends Ben and Gwen Gimson, a lovely couple, Ben being a member of the county committee.

Arriving at the ground I was intrigued to find Norman enjoying a cup of coffee and conversation with a number of young ladies occupying a camper van beyond the boundary. When he left the van and returned to the pavilion just before start of play, Gwen and I decided to have a walk round the ground. Eventually we arrived at the camper van and Gwen knocked on the door, popped her head inside and addressed the young ladies thus: 'I think it's time you should meet Mrs McVicker!' Deathly hush for a few seconds before we were invited inside for a welcome 'cuppa' and a chat, and the cards and letters continued thereafter for a number of years, until the girls got older and wiser!

****

Bernard Thomas
International gymnast, physiotherapist and mentor on
many England tours

I was very privileged to travel all over the world in my role with the England cricket team, which also meant acting as medical adviser, assistant manager, father confessor and occasionally head chef, particularly in up-country India, where a diet of eggs and chips or beans on toast was infinitely preferable to some of the dubious-looking curries on offer! I came into contact with people from all walks of life, many of whom I still count as good friends today, and have particularly good memories of the youngsters in every country and their enthusiasm for the sport of cricket, whether it was played on the beaches in the West Indies or in the intervals in front of a capacity crowd in Calcutta. I have a lovely photograph of Bob Taylor, whilst on a post-tour holiday in Kashmir, joining in with an impromptu game and keeping wicket for the local lads behind a tombstone in the graveyard!

However, my tale is not from my touring experiences but from my days of coaching my first sport of gymnastics. As a result of this I was asked to coach students at the Queen Alexandra College for the Blind in Birmingham, many of whom were not only blind but had other physical handicaps, and to be able to get them on a trampoline and generally moving with confidence was a very rewarding experience for us all.

Among the group were a number of lads from Pakistan, who needless to say were mad on their cricket, and one day I organised an 'England versus Pakistan' Test match for them. There were of course certain modifications called for, such as an 'audible' ball, either a wicker ball containing pebbles or one made from tin so that the lads could hear its position. There was a ruling that the ball had to bounce twice before reaching the wicket.

All went well until towards the end of the match when 'England' were batting and the 'Pakistan' team captain announced he was changing the bowlers and putting his 'quickie' on. I immediately heard a cry from the facing batsman and on going over to see what he wanted, was told he wished to appeal against the light!

A very amusing, but at the same time humbling experience.

****

Arthur Fairchild
Member, Middlesex CCC

On entering Lord's pavilion one day I overheard a doorman state to a visitor, 'I am sorry sir, you cannot enter the pavilion without wearing a tie.'

Visitor's response, 'But you have just let in David Nixon without hair!'

****

Doug Insole CBE
Essex CCC, England

About 50 years ago, Warwickshire were playing Essex at Colchester and most of the first day was spent waiting around for the ground to dry.

It was not, as it happened, time completely wasted because the opportunity was taken to resolve a little argument, and a few bets, that had been cooking nicely over several weeks in the Warwickshire dressing room. It all revolved about whether Ray Hitchcock, the quickest over the ground in the Warwickshire side, could concede 'yards for years' to the slowest, Eric Hollies, and beat him over 100 yards.

The age difference was 17 years and in consequence Eric was to be given 17 yards start. The reason that I, the opposing captain, was involved in the situation was that feelings and wagers were running so high that a neutral person was required to measure out the distances and act as adjudicator for the contest.

Actually, it was no contest. Eric won comfortably. Ray Hitchcock caught up several yards but was still well adrift at the finish. His mistake was not to specify that his opponent should run 100 yards and he would run 117 yards, because Eric was fairly knackered after his 83 yard journey.

Quite a decent crowd watched the race and a fair bit of cash changed hands. What is certain is that the bookie, the wily Jack Bannister, ended up a few bob on the right side. For my part, I was relieved it was not a close finish. The Edgbaston mob could turn quite nasty when provoked!

Those, as they say, were the days.

****

Bill McVicker
Stand CC

After his county career my brother Norman returned to play a few games for his old club. Local press had featured his impending return which added quite a few spectators at the gate. Stand fielded first and Norman opened the bowling with me at the other end and after half a dozen overs and fielding at third man, I overhead the following conversation between two elderly spectators: 'Which one is this Norman McVicker, then?' His companion replied, 'It must be this chap here. T'other bugger's doing nowt!'

****

Barry Hardcastle
Oldham CC

When we were youngsters we could not wait for net practice nights, mingling and learning from the older, senior, players - who would always spare a word of encouragement to those keen to learn - just basically bowling to them, retrieving balls from the outfield, studying them and then perhaps getting your pads on for a few deliveries in fading light! And on match days, helping the scorer by maintaining the scoreboard and hoping for a free tea as reward.

Selection meetings were on Monday evenings in the pavilion to choose next week-end's teams. As youngsters we would admire the names on the notice board and dread one day your name would appear on the lists. Later, entering the changing room on a match day for the very first time was daunting, but the seniors and others made you welcome, understanding your nervousness.

We all had good and bad days as, hopefully, we progressed through the 2nd X1 to the dizzy heights of the 1st X1. Down the years I am sure we all enjoyed the game, at whatever level, and despite our individual 'ups' and 'downs'.

Now where are we? Lounging around the boundary in deckchairs or in the bar, beer in hand, perhaps with a bit of a paunch, easily commenting on what is going on the field: 'He's not much of a spin bowler, is he?'- 'Why has the captain still got that man at point?'- 'No third slip!'- 'Should get the fast bowler back on at this end!' etc.

We old players must encourage young players as much as possible and I hope that, in our various ways, we do. 'Tis worth remembering, as I do very clearly, the words of an old North American Indian saying: *'Let me not criticise my neighbour until I have walked ten miles in his moccasins.'*

Perhaps worth remembering in our dotage.......

****

Rachel Heyhoe-Flint MBE
Captain England Ladies X1

My first tour with England was to South Africa in 1960, travelling by ship - SS Pretoria Castle, part of the Union Castle Line. We were meant to practice daily on board, but made sure we 'lost' all practice balls overboard before we had passed the Isle of Wight!

Arrived at Cape Town after two weeks of sociabilities on board to be greeted by South African officials, who told us they had arranged a 'Welcome Dinner Dance' the following night. Our manager was anxious and said we hadn't any partners for the occasion - remember this was 1960 and a rather formal occasion!

Our hosts replied, 'Don't worry about not having partners - we've advertised for you in the local paper!'

****

Bill Beaumont
England Rugby Captain

One of my favourite stories is the one of the Irish Rugby Team arriving in Fiji in the 70's for an International match only to find the Fijians had already left on another tour!

****

Tony Bamber
Prestwich CC

The captain of our first X1 returned to the pavilion after the toss for innings. Our 'pro' asked him if we were batting, or in the field. Gerry Blight, the captain and a softly- spoken man, answered him whereupon the 'pro' padded up with his fellow opener. Shortly afterwards, they were sitting outside the pavilion ready for the start of play and noticed two of the opposition sitting with pads on, bats and gloves ready for the hostilities.
It took some diplomacy to resolve the situation and get the game under way.

****

Bill McVicker
Stand CC

The Reverend Jonathon Jennings was curate to the Bishop of Manchester. As such, he did not have a parish but took services around the area as required. He was also an enthusiastic cricketer, playing for our 3rd X1 as a bowler.
One Sunday afternoon during the tea interval, a spectator suggested to him he was cutting it close if he was to preach at a local church at 6.30pm. Jonathon, for whatever reason, was totally unaware of this call on his professional services.
After explaining the situation to our skipper he, our regular

number eleven, was instructed to open our batting, get on with it and then get out!

To the team's delight, every stroke produced runs and he raced to his highest score for the club before engineering his own dismissal. The church organist had played the opening Hymn several times before he arrived in the pulpit with his surplice covering his whites!

****

Colin Kennedy
Crusaders CC

It was a Saturday afternoon and I was captain of the side playing Paper Mills at their then splendid ground in Littlefield Lane. Bruce Robinson was bowling from the pavilion end and a certain character called Peter Griffiths was fielding at first slip. Three balls had been bowled when my eagle eye spotted Peter putting his hand in his trousers' pocket and pulling out a packet of Woodbines. Unbelievably he removed one of the cigarettes, put it in his mouth, took out a box of matches and lit up.

Promptly I stopped Bruce from starting his run up and said, 'Peter, you either put that cigarette out, or leave the field.' To the amazement of his team mates and myself, he replied, 'If it's all right with you skip I'll leave the field,' and off he went!

Sadly, Peter died some five years ago and I attended his funeral.

****

At the end of the Second World War the Crusaders were invited to play at Cuxwold in a Sunday friendly. No changing facilities were available in those days, but we had an extended tea interval by going to the homes of our opponents. My story involves the captain, Dick Walgate, who bowled down the slope from which end his father umpired. The difficult bit was to keep your pads out of the way of the ball. Eventually you were unsuccessful, with Dick turning to his father shouting, 'How's that dad?' In a flash the finger would be raised followed by the dreaded words 'You're out, well bowled son!' Happy days.

****

Robin Jackman
Surrey CCC and England

I don't know why Cleethorpes Cricket Club should remind me of a benefit match years ago in the south of England, when I captained a Surrey side for the beneficiary whose name, through complete loss of memory, escapes me.

We fielded first in order to control the game as best we could, giving a few runs here, stopping the flow of runs there, until the automatic declaration at the tea interval.

Whilst the wives and girlfriends of the opposing team were duly laying out the cucumber sandwiches and chocolate cake, the groundsman, who appeared to be many years older than the club, came to me and said, 'Now then Mr Jackman, what roller would you like on this 'ere wicket? Would you like the light roller, the 'eavy roller or the only bleeding roller we've got?

****

Dr. Ali Bacher
Transvaal and South Africa

I believe I am the only cricketer ever to have scored three ducks in a first-class cricket match.

The match was between Transvaal and Western Province. The events were as follows:

On New Year's Day, I lost the toss for the first time in 17 matches. Eddie Barlow, the opposing captain, elected to bat and was top scorer with 76 in a total of 326. The following day, with the 'house full' signs up, 'Bubbles' Bath and myself opened the Transvaal reply. The fast bowler John Cawood was bowling with the new ball into the wind. Ali hit the ball hard and it flew like a bullet to gully where Richard Morris took the catch. Out for a duck in a disappointing total of 197. The next day was the traditional rest day, and it saw the mischievous Coghill taking bets around the country that his captain would bag a pair for the first time in his career.

The following day again facing Cawood, this time bowling from the opposite end, Ali edged him to Hylton Ackerman fielding at second slip before he had opened his score. The ball went to him. He claimed a catch and they all appealed. There was a cloud of dust gusting around, so I wasn't certain he had taken a clean catch. I wasn't going to walk unless I was sure. So I stuck around and the umpire said, 'Not out.' There was a lot of chat directed at me from the close fielders and 'Bubbles' walked down to my end. 'You okay?' he asked.

'Bubbles recalls: 'There was a bit of stand-off between him (Ali) and Barlow - you could say they were vigorously competitive - and I went to give him some moral support - and he said to me he was to me was okay and he'd be alright now.' The next ball, however, was edged again and this time Bacher was caught fair and square by Andre Bruyns.

'Ali looked down the wicket at me and winked with both eyes. That was Ali, he always winked with both eyes at the same time!'

Bacher continues, 'As I walked off the ground, I spotted a beaming Coghill at the top of the dressing room stairs applauding very loudly every step of the way.' 'Well done, I'm proud of you!' he said.

After the match, Ackerman told me the catch he had taken was a fair one. The ball had hit his boot and popped into his hands. Ali confronted Coghill. 'You can say what you like. I'm the first player to be bag a pair and be dismissed three times for nought in a first-class match!'

****

Ray Mawer
President, Cleethorpes CC

There is always confusion when the fielding side attempt a run out when the bails have already been dislodged. In a match some years ago between Gloucestershire and Sussex, it was mega confusion! Ron Nicholls and David Carpenter were batting for Gloucestershire. David played a ball to cover. Ron ran - David did not. Result, both men at the striker's end having a few words with each other!

At the other end the bowler, Tony Buss, had collected the ball but in doing so had dislodged the bails. He picked the ball up, looked uncertainly at the umpire and enquired, 'What do I do now?' 'Don't ask me, lad!' was the only reply. He desperately called to his skipper at slip. 'Pull the stump up', he shouted. Transferring the ball to his left hand, Tony triumphantly pulled out a stump with his right. 'How's that?' he yelled. 'Not out.' Tony grabbed another stump and hurled it into the middle distance. 'Not out' said the umpire with infuriating calmness. By now, Tony had completely lost it and turned to his captain - by now foaming at the mouth. 'Pull the f...... thing out with the hand that's holding ball.' This he did, triumphantly raising the last stump above his head and shouting, 'Well, how is that then?' 'Not out. The batter's behind you, lad, been there for five minutes!'

Tony's day of misfortune was not over. His wife arrived on the ground just at that moment and seeing her husband towering over the diminutive umpire, apparently threatening him with a stump, shouted out from the pavilion, 'Tony, don't you dare hit that poor little man!'

****

Steve Boulton
East Halton CC, local and MCCA umpire

'Some of the problems of umpiring'
You often witness a batsman being hit in the box, for want of a better description, and we all know how it feels! On one occasion it happened to me when I was umpiring - and wasn't wearing one - as you think you are safe in the white coat.
It happened to me at Skegness and as the bowler's arm came over, the ball slipped out of his hand and caught me fair and square. (I bet he could not give a repeat performance if he tried!) Needless to say, both teams thought it was hilarious, which was more than I did, when I inspected the 'damage' after the game!
You may have read that in one of last year's first-class matches, the teams were obliged to leave the field because the sun was blinding the players and they had to wait for it to move round. It once happened to me when standing in a minor counties game at March some four years ago. As the sun got lower it came straight through a gap in the buildings and into the face of the batsman. The umpires had no alternative but to take the players off until it went further round.

****

Tim Lamb
Oxford University, Middlesex and Northamptonshire CCC, TCCB

I am not sure how many times I played against Yorkshire, but will never forget some of the fun and games that went in the margins of those contests!
Like the time that John Hampshire and his brother, Colin, went on a batting 'go slow' at Northampton in protest at Geoffrey Boycott having yet again taken 90 out of the statutory 100 overs to score a century.
Like the time when the start of the game at Scarborough was

held up by picketing pensioners and handbag-waving old ladies protesting about Boycott's suspension and banishment from the dressing room for speaking out of turn to the press.

Or the time when Chris Old was relieved of the captaincy during our match at Middlesbrough, which led to further tensions in an already volatile Yorkshire dressing room. During the same match the then Yorkshire physio, the notorious Eric 'the Beast' was manhandled, kicking and roaring, into the communal bath, virtually emptying all the water!

But my favourite recollection of playing against the Tykes is a match which took place in The Parks in the early '70s when, with the University nine wickets down in the second innings and about ten minutes to go to the close, with the extra half-hour having been claimed by Yorkshire in anticipation of a two-day victory over the students, muggins (who in those days did not know one end of the bat from the other) walked out to bat with instructions to at least save some face by making the game go into the third day.

Boycs, the captain, wanted to go home. All the rest of the Yorkshire team wanted to stay on an extra night to enjoy the varied distractions of an Oxford summer evening. For ten priceless minutes we had the spectacle of Geoff Cope trying as hard as he could not to get me out, and of David 'Bluey' Bairstow coaching me - pleading with me - from behind the stumps. (Stick your front leg down the wicket son; leave this one; bat behind pad lad; don't for eff's sake cut against the spin!)

Somehow I survived the last four overs or so. The Yorkshire lads virtually chaired me off the field. Boycott was absolutely spitting. At least some dark blue honour had been saved and Bluey and Co (I assume) had their riotous night on the town!

**

A favourite recollection of your editor? The time when, sitting in the player's viewing room at Edgbaston on a very wet day, he read aloud from 'Mayfair' magazine as if it were a Jane Austin novel!

****

Mike Drew
Chairman, Cleethorpes CC

The incident concerns a wicketkeeper for a team called Grimsby Amateurs who later played for Cleethorpes for a while. His name was Jack Croft-Baker, later Sir Jack, who was a leading figure on Grimsby Docks. Like many 'keepers, he was small in stature and liked to stand up to the stumps when possible.
The match in question was a Grimsby Town KO match, 20 overs a side in those days. Although the bowler was above fast-medium, Jack was standing up to the stumps, with his nose nearly touching the wicket, to deter the batsman from advancing down the pitch. The batsman was then bowled, only for one of the bails to lodge in Jack's forehead.
He was escorted from the field and on arrival at the pavilion, the bail was removed with quite a loss of blood over his shirt and kit.
I don't recall the result of the match but I shall always remember the incident.

****

Rosemary McVicker

'Just a touch of nostalgia'
My father rented Glebe Farm in Yarburgh, near Louth, in his early days. The farmhouse was immediately adjacent the church. They were the happiest of days and I well remember helping my mother clean the church every week even though I

was only three or four years old.

On occasion, mum and dad would go off to a whist drive, leaving me in the tender care of Mr Bert Bratley, a farm labourer employed by my father for many years, who would act as 'baby-sitter'.

A kindly man, Bert used to read to me to help pass the time and I well recall one evening, with Bert ensconced in a comfy chair near the fire and me standing by his side as he read from a book entitled 'The Three Little Pigs'.

Looking at the illustrations, I asked him why one of the pigs had a patch in his trousers. 'That's not a patch. It's a winder', he replied. Somewhat confused, I asked why he needed a winder (window) in his trousers, to which Bert replied, 'So he can see what's going on inside'.

That was nearly seventy years ago! I recall Bert Bratley fondly and I still have the book on The Three Little Pigs!

****

Peter Wheeler
Leicester 'Tigers' RUFC and England

'Balmy days'

In the dim and distant past I played for England against Tonga in their beautiful group of islands in the Pacific. It was in June 1979 and Tonga away is a fixture that any self-respecting rugby player should jump at. Wonderful hospitality, natural beaches and the opportunity to witness a totally different culture.

I had the opportunity to captain England because Bill Beaumont had been injured playing against Fiji, another worthwhile away trip, and so I had the honour of introducing the England team before the match to the King of Tonga, who as his status and 28-stone dictated, remained at the top of the main and only stand, and we all trooped up there to shake his hand.

The trickiest part of the day was when the groundsman could

not find the key to the padlock on the dressing rooms and had to knock it off with a hammer. Once he had taken his bicycle out of our dressing room, we could get changed.

The King's nephew, if I remember rightly, played on the wing - or I think anywhere else he liked to play! In the match we finished off the tour nicely with a 37-17 victory, Mike Slemen scoring two tries. But the sheer beauty of the island, the hospitality and the occasion itself is something which remains close to my heart.

****

By kind permission of **Michael Parkinson CBE**
From his book 'Michael Parkinson on Cricket'.

'Those who stand and serve'
I remember my first umpire well. His name was Jim Smith and he always took his teeth out before a game. I never discovered why but I always supposed it was a safety precaution due to the state of our wickets and the ferocity of our cricket.

He was a marvellous man, tall and dignified even without his teeth, with an infallible technique for puncturing swollen heads. I remember as a youngster playing well and scoring 50 or so in a game he was umpiring. I carried my bat and as I came off the field, triumphant, imagining myself to be an unbelievable mixture of Bradman and Hutton, he joined me at my shoulder. As we walked in together, I looked towards him anticipating a word of praise. He glanced sidelong at me and out of the corner of his mouth said, 'Does tha' want some advice, lad?'
I said I did.
'Well get thi' bloody hair cut,' he said.
Two matches later he gave me out lbw and as I walked sullenly past him he said, out of the corner of his toothless mouth, 'If tha'd get thi' bloody hair cut tha'd stop them balls wi' thi' bat.'
Jim Smith was my introduction to that delightful body of men, the cricket umpire. I can think of no other group that does so

much for so little. By comparison the soccer referee is a pampered ninny, and the fact that cricket has survived this far without requiring the umpires to take the field without carrying truncheons says much for their character. The secret, of course, is their humour. There are few funny stories about soccer or rugby referees and anyone who tells me a funny about a tennis umpire will receive a gold-plated pig by return of post. But there is a Bumper Fun Book of Funny Umpire Stories.

Many of them concern Alec Skelding. My favourite Skelding story concerns the aggrieved batsman who, on being out lbw, addressed Skelding thus:

'Where's your white stick umpire?'

'Left it at home,' said Alec.

'What about your guide dog?' said the batsman.

'Got rid of it for yappin' same as I'm getting rid of you,' replied Skelding.

Joe Hayes never rose to Skelding's heights in cricket but in the local league I played in as a youth he was just as big a legend. Those who knew Joe well always appealed for everything as opening time approached because Joe had a job as a waiter in a local boozer and had to be duty at 6pm. It was his proud boast that he had never been late at the boozer in twenty years, and could produce several hundred cursing batsmen to bear him witness. His other quirk was a dislike of loud appealing. He himself rarely raised his voice above a murmur and his face creased in pain and disgust whenever a bowler bellowed in his earhole.

We had in our team at the time the best appealer of all time. His voice rattled windows several miles away and set dogs to whimpering. This particular game his raucous appeals finally got on Joe's nerves. After one particularly loud one Joe could stand it no longer.

'Owz-that!' bellowed the bowler.

'Not out,' Joe bellowed back in an even louder voice. The bowler stood amazed that Joe should raise his voice.

'I'm only bloody askin' thi',' he said in a pained voice.

'Ay, and I'm bloody tellin' thi',' shouted Joe.

All of which leads to Cec Pepper, who as a player in the Lancashire League was renowned as much for his verbal battles with umpires as he was for his cricketing prowess.

Pepper was the scourge of Lancashire League umpires, blasting the meek with his belligerent appealing, making the lay preachers blush with his vivid language. The umpire who faced up to him had to be a special kind of human being and George Long was such a man.

George was standing one day at the end where Pepper was bowling, when Pepper made one of his raucous Australian appeals for lbw, which was answered by a quiet 'Not out.' Whereupon Pepper gave vent to a histrionic stream of invective throwing in all the stock-in-trade props - spectacles, white stick, guide dog, illegitimacy, bloody-minded Englishness and four letter words - all of which George completely ignored.

The same thing happened after the next ball and yet again after the following one, after which George called 'Over' and walked to his square-leg position, followed by Pepper - obviously disturbed by the lack of reaction from the umpire.

'I suppose you're going to report all this bad language to the League?' said Pepper.

'No,' replied George. 'Ah likes a man as speaks his mind.' Pepper was obviously delighted.

'So do I' he said smiling, and I must say it's a refreshing change to meet an umpire like you. I'm glad we understand each other.

'Aye,' said George.

The first ball of the next over again hit the batsman's pads, whereupon Cec whirled round to George, arms outstretched and did his usual Red Indian war-whoop. His 'Owzat' was heard all round the ground.

'Not out, you fat Australian bastard,' said George quietly.

****

Martin Maslin
Cleethorpes CC, Lincolnshire CCC and MCCA

'A 'Hot' reception'
I well recall my debut for the Minor Counties X1 against the
West Indies in 1966. Bill Edrich captained the team in a two-
day match at the Lakenham ground in Norwich.
Put into bat by Rohan Kanhai, Wes Hall bowled a superb spell
to return 7 for 31 as the Minor Counties were demolished for a
paltry 65 before lunch. I had never seen a slip cordon placed so
deep, in fact they must have been half-way to the boundary
rope! I did not entirely enjoy my own time at the crease in the
first innings - and was not alone in that!!
Unfortunately, Fred Millett, the Cheshire captain and a good
player, was hit on the hand by 'Wes' and suffered a crushed
knuckle in the process ruling him out of the game. In fact, I did
see his hand later in the day after hospitalisation and only three
knuckles were visible! We were totally outplayed and lost by
and innings and 33 runs. But I remember Kanhai easing up
with his bowlers in the second innings, thereby enabling one or
two of us to accumulate a few runs!

****

'A first-class debut'
I was included in the side to play against Pakistan the
following year at Swindon, when Intikhab claimed twelve
wickets and we lost by only 23 runs in a very good and close
run contest. Whilst I did manage a half-century in our second
innings, from close up it was intriguing to see a top-class slow
bowler at work. 'Inty' bowled his leg-spinners and googlies
rather faster than Johnny Lawrence who 'teased' many batsmen
with his slow bowling - with an alert Ron Beeson behind the
stumps - and who served Lincolnshire so well in the
fifties/sixties.
I do recall the Pakistanis were a friendly side and Asif Iqbal,
who was much taken with my team-mate Norman McVicker's

boots. I subsequently learned they were made by a cobbler in Northampton, a Mr Whiting, who supplied many first-class players with boots made from kangaroo skin. I believe Asif, then only a young man who subsequently played with much distinction for his country and Kent, immediately ordered at least a pair. Like many other players, he was saddened when Mr Whiting retired from his business and moved to Canada some ten years later.

****

Sue Monger
Thatcham, Berkshire

'The honourable seamstress'
One day, when a seamstress was sewing while sitting close to a river, her thimble fell into the water.
When she cried out, the Lord appeared and asked, 'My dear child, why are you crying?'
The seamstress replied that her thimble had fallen into the river and she needed it to help her husband in making a living for their family.
The Lord dipped his hand into the water and pulled out a golden thimble set with pearls.
'Is this your thimble?' asked the Lord. The seamstress replied, 'No.'
The Lord again dipped into the river. He held out a silver thimble. 'Is this your thimble?' the Lord asked. Again, the seamstress replied, 'No.'
The Lord reached down again and came up with a leather thimble. 'Is this your thimble?' the Lord asked. The seamstress replied, 'Yes.'
The Lord was pleased with the woman's honesty and gave her all three thimbles to keep, and the seamstress went home happy.
Some years later, the seamstress and her husband were walking along the riverbank when her husband fell into the water and

disappeared.

When she cried out, the Lord again appeared and asked her, 'Why are you crying?' 'Oh Lord, my husband has fallen into the water!'

The Lord went down into the water and came up with George Clooney. 'Is this your husband?' he asked. 'Yes,' cried the seamstress. The Lord was furious. 'You lied! That was an untruth!'

The seamstress replied, 'Oh, forgive me, my Lord it is a misunderstanding. You see, if I had said 'No' to George Clooney, you would have come up with Brad Pitt. Then if I said 'No' to him, you would have come up with my husband. Had I then said 'Yes' you would have given me all three. Lord, I'm not in the best of health and would not be able to take care of all three husbands, so THAT'S why I said 'yes' to George Clooney.'

And so the Lord let her keep him.

The moral of this story is: Whenever a woman lies, it's for a good and honourable reason and in the interests of others......!

****

Mike Povall
Prestwick CC, Lancashire ground-staff

'Recollections'
Cliff Gladwin, a fine Derbyshire and England bowler, came out to bat at Old Trafford with Derbyshire struggling, seven wickets down, and Brian Statham creating havoc!
I was on duty by the players gate and the pitch was right on the far side of the Old Trafford square. As I opened the gate, Gladwin gazed into the distance, then, turning to me asked 'Have you got a bicycle?' He then strode to the middle but returned after one ball; bowled Statham 'nought'. He remarked in a loud voice as he mounted the pavilion steps, 'That was a bloody long way for nowt!'

****

A certain Dr. Burstock, a full member of the county club with connections within the committee – he played in the Manchester Association, a slightly elitist organisation in those days – and was allowed to join the senior players in net practice from time to time.
This particular day he was facing Tommy Greenhough, a fine leg spinner, as I passed the net. 'Tommy' I said, 'give me the ball'. (In those days I bowled slow left arm). Tommy obliged and I ran in an imitation of Greenhough's approach and delivery which completely flummoxed the doctor, the ball pitching a foot outside off-stump on a perfect length and ripping back to take his leg stump. (A bit like Shane Warne's magnificent leg spinner to dismiss Mike Gatting in that famous Test.)
To me it was the chinaman of all chinamen and easily the best ball I ever bowled.

****

Jack Ikin was my favourite cricketer and I remember him with much affection. Left-hand batsman, who played 18 Tests for England, he was stylish with strokes all around the wicket, but I remember his execution of the late cut most of all. Delicate to say the least and most effective. Once he gave me a pair of his cricket boots which I treasured and wore for several seasons when playing for the Prestwich club.

A story is told that Jack, following an early game for the England XI, somehow left his England sweater overnight at Old Trafford on one of the comfortable cinema seats in the home dressing room – arranged then in two tiers, visiting teams having to put up with a single row. Arriving next morning he discovered the pavilion cat had chosen to have a litter of five kittens on his sweater! Somewhat cap in hand, he had to approach Lords for a replacement; no doubt granted.

****

Tim Marsh
Somerset & Rochdale

'The 10 minute game'
The Benson & Hedges Group 'A' table on the morning of Thursday, 24th May in 1979 was thus:

	P	W	L	D	Pts
Somerset	3	3	0	0	9
Worcester	3	2	1	0	6
Glamorgan	3	2	1	0	6
Gloucester	4	1	3	0	3
M Counties	3	0	3	0	0

Two teams from the regional group would qualify for the quarter final play-offs. Should any two teams finish level on points, the outcome would be decided on bowling strike rate.
Somerset were certain to qualify unless Worcester beat them that day, AND Glamorgan beat Minor Counties, AND (wait for

it) both significantly increased their bowling strike rate over Somerset's.

There had been bad weather that week which ruled out play on the Wednesday so, with an uncertain forecast for Thursday, the Somerset captain, Brian Rose, hatched a plan and declared the Somerset innings after a single over, thereby placing Somerset in a losing position.

The '10 minute game' (not including the break between innings) produced 3 runs from 17 balls – done entirely to protect Somerset's strike rate. More than unusual but perfectly legal at the time. There were about a hundred paying spectators at Taunton that day who were more than a little upset!

On 1st June the TCCB ruled that Somerset be expelled from that season's competition for 'not complying with the spirit of the game'. Essex eventually won that season's B&H trophy and very shortly after an alteration to the rules was introduced to prevent any recurrence of Somerset's deliberate ploy!

Somerset went on to win the B&H trophy twice in the following three years.

ISBN 978-142690005-1